STREET SMARTS FOR KIDS

WHAT PARENTS MUST KNOW TO KEEP THEIR CHILDREN SAFE

STREET
SMARTS
FOR KIDS

WHAT PARENTS MUST KNOW TO KEEP THEIR CHILDREN SAFE

Detective Ric Bentz and Christine Allison

FAWCETT BOOKS THE BALLANTINE PUBLISHING GROUP NEW YORK

A Fawcett Book
Published by The Ballantine Publishing Group

www.randomhouse.com/BB/

Library of Congress Cataloging-in-Publication Data
Bentz, Ric.
Street smarts for kids : what parents must know to keep their
children safe / Ric Bentz and Christine Allison.
    p.   cm.
Includes index.
ISBN: 0-449-91237-X   (alk. paper)
1. Children—United States—Life skills guides. 2. Parenting—United States.
3. Social skills in children. I. Allison, Christine. II. Title.
HQ792.U5 B46   1999
649'.1—dc21
                              99-24417

Text design by Holly Johnson

Cover design by Jennifer Blanc
Cover photo © Spencer Rowell/FPG International

Manufactured in the United States of America

First Edition: October 1999
10 9 8 7 6 5 4 3

This book is dedicated to all children,
but especially Chrissie Allison
and others like her with special needs,
in hopes that, someday, with proper training,
they, too, can live life without fear.

Anecdotes based upon real cases are used to illustrate the safety methods described in this book. In those instances where facts about a case are not a matter of public record, the names have been changed to protect the privacy of the victims.

Contents

Acknowledgments

Many people made this book possible. First, I would like to thank my wife, Pam, and my sons, Jason and Nick, for their years of love, support, and understanding.

I am also grateful to a number of my associates:

To former Chief of Police Gerald Schuetz for giving me the opportunity to really help children;

To Chief of Police Dan Wade for his years of experience and understanding that gave me the ability and opportunity to finish this project;

To Lt. Paula Mickelsen, my mentor and my friend, for her expert tutelage in the field of child sexual abuse;

To Dr. Stephen Lazoritz for his endless medical knowledge and his willingness to take time to answer questions about child safety;

To Brian Holmgren for challenging me to become a better investigator with his insights and investigative techniques;

To Lt. Thomas Cerqua, Community Relations officer, for the use of his material and experience;

ACKNOWLEDGMENTS

To Officer Friendly, Dennis Walsh, for all of his help with the Street Smart Kid Program;

To Mr. Daniel J. Travanti for what he does to help us teach our children to be safe.

I would like to thank Patty Brown and John Boswell for their help agenting the book. And finally—and especially—Elisa Wares at The Ballantine Publishing Group. It's been tremendous to have an editor who so clearly cares about the welfare of children.

STREET SMARTS FOR KIDS

WHAT PARENTS MUST KNOW TO KEEP THEIR CHILDREN SAFE

WELCOME TO MY WORLD

Most people think of Kenosha, Wisconsin, as the perfect American town. Trees line the streets, the public schools are good, and the neighbors are friendly. Recently, *Reader's Digest* named Kenosha one of the top ten cities in the country. As part of that ranking, we were described as one of the safest places in America to raise children.

Unfortunately, as a detective in the sensitive crimes unit, I see another side of Kenosha.

Here, in a town that could have come right out of a Frank Capra movie, are everyday folks—or at least people who seem that way—who routinely abuse children. Here, even among "good" families, are children who disappear or run away from home or are kidnapped.

Fear isn't supposed to be part of any childhood, and I didn't write this book to make you or your children afraid. But unless you as a parent are aware and educated, I can tell you right now, your child is at risk. As a police officer who has seen a lot over the past twenty years, I can tell you that the current generation of children is facing new and

difficult assaults on their safety and well-being. With predators chatting with children on the Internet and sexual and
physical abuse at an all-time high, parents absolutely must
take extraordinary steps to train their children in how to
be safe. If our little community can keep four other detec-
tives and me running day and night to rescue children and
investigate and prevent crimes against them, you need to
ask yourself what is happening in your town. Ask your
police chief to give you the facts. I can promise you will be
shocked.

A POLICE OFFICER'S POINT OF VIEW

A lot of parents think crimes against children are random
and pretty much unavoidable. I call it the "there but for the
grace of God go I" approach. That approach is indefensible.
In the vast majority of cases, most of the abductions and
abuse cases could be avoided if children and parents knew
what to do. As a matter of fact, most accidents involving
child safety could be avoided if *children* knew what to do.
My purpose is to help you train your child to be street smart
and practical about everything from avoiding sexual abuse
to crossing the street.

Many wonderful people are helping to fight the battle to
keep our children safe. We all have different approaches. I
am not a safety educator. I am not a child psychologist. I am
not a social worker. I am a front-line cop who deals with the
predators, the victims, and the families every day of the
year. I have learned a lot about the kind of people who do

horrible things to children. I have learned a lot about how children think and react—and what kinds of behavior put them in most jeopardy. I don't have a lot of long-winded theories and I'm not going to drag you through a lot of horror stories. I am going to tell you the real way all of this works. Then, with some simple guidelines, I am going to show you how to train your child to be safe.

Street smarts is a mind-set. Once you train your child, he or she will know how to respond to danger. This kind of training will not only keep your child safe from sick adults but will help your child avoid unnecessary accidents. It will help him know what to do if he smells smoke or sustains a deep wound.

This book, read once and used well, could literally save your child's life.

SITTING DUCKS

If you think that teaching your child streets smarts is just another afterschool activity, I need to clarify the matter. Child safety isn't an option, like tennis or piano lessons. It's life or death. Without a certain kind of street smarts, your child is a sitting duck.

Throughout my career, I've worked with children all over the Midwest. On the face of it, they seem sophisticated. They can whiz around the Internet (a subject we'll get to in Chapter 7). They are exposed to the kind of television and radio programming that should be for adults only. Their clothes are hot, their talk is smart. But in reality, these children suffer from either too much or too little in-dependence, which puts them at the mercy of predators.

Inner-city kids have too much independence. They grow up too fast. I've worked with thousands of city kids, and the children who seem so tough are really just *playing* tough. My city kids are dealing with poverty and single-parent house-holds, and they don't get the supervision or guidance they need. What I have to offer them is common sense, the kind of smarts that can save lives.

The suburban kids, on the other hand, seem to have too *little* independence. They can't go to the park without an adult. They can't go to a friend's house unless someone drives them there. Their lives are crammed with afterschool lessons and activities. In the 1990s, through no fault of his own, the suburban child lives in a bubble. He has had little independent contact with the world and has made too few decisions on his own. Some kids barely know how to walk to school.

Unlike children of previous generations, these children will not develop common sense naturally. They need to be trained.

Let's start with *your* child. Your child needs you to make his safety a priority. As a police officer, I can say that one of the biggest stumbling blocks to raising strong, confident, street-smart children is the parents themselves. Concern about your child's safety is not paranoia or obsessiveness. It's realistic.

Fact one: *Parents, not teachers, are responsible for safety instruction.* Safety training is one aspect of your child's edu-cation you can't delegate. While 88 percent of all elementary schools have some kind of safety program, they don't have the time or resources to provide more than an overview. There are no afterschool "safety clubs," or safety tutors or safety camps. Safety, common sense, street smarts—call it what you will—must be passed on to children by their parents.

This doesn't mean that you are responsible for every bite or scratch or accident that befalls your child. It means that without you as a teacher, your child will go through life without the practical tools he needs to respond to danger.

Fact two: *In many ways, modern children lack the common sense of previous generations.* Not only are you fully responsible for this kind of training, but the job has gotten harder. Earlier in this century, children were expected to acquire practical skills—sewing or milking cows or fixing faucets—as a matter of routine. The modern child, by contrast, is often ignorant in practical matters. He does not have a hands-on sense of the world and he is often clueless when it comes to processing danger signals or trouble. Thus training must be more intensive than it might have been twenty or thirty years ago.

Fact three: *Children who are constantly protected from the real world are less equipped to live in it.* Being a street-smart parent doesn't mean setting up a fortress to shield your child from the world. It means teaching your child how to live in the world with confidence. It also means letting your child fail and make mistakes and suffer consequences. Parents, especially those in suburbia, too often rescue their children, whether it means fetching a forgotten lunch sack or funding the teen who is always running out of money.

Discussing the concept of danger with a child who has been protected in this manner is extremely difficult.

All of this talk about danger doesn't mean your child needs to purchase his wardrobe at the army-navy store. It simply means that you need to acknowledge and discuss the reality of danger. As you work with your child using the ideas in this book, stress that for the most part, people are good and decent. We just need to be alert to the handful of people who do not have our best interests at heart.

Remember, if Kenosha, Wisconsin has enough crime to keep me and my coworkers busy, you can believe that wherever you live, it's happening near you.

Chapter 1

TEACHING STREET SMARTS

A Coast Guard officer was giving a demonstration on water safety to a group of ten-year-old campers. He lit a flare and, thinking it had burned out, tossed it into a pile of leaves. While he animatedly continued with his talk, a fire developed in the leaf pile behind him. The children—too polite to interrupt—said nothing. By the time the officer noticed the fire, it was out of control.

Doubtless, these children had good manners. They had "don't interrupt" down pat, but they had no street smarts. They were unable to respond spontaneously and intelligently to fire, an obvious, visible danger. But these children are not unusual. In fact, many children are lacking in modern-day common sense. They have not had the repetition and practice that is required when learning street smarts. Street smarts can't be learned in a single sitting; it will not sink in from an isolated lesson on the blackboard or a video presentation alone.

Unlike other kinds of intelligence, street smarts must come from training, rather than educating. Training is what we do in police and fire departments and in the armed services. We rehearse a response to a particular situation over and over again. We establish principles that will help us make on-the-spot decisions. If you are a street-smart parent, you need to be able to think ahead and anticipate situations your child might find himself or herself in. You need to establish an appropriate response. And then you have to come up with the 101 exceptions to that response and acquaint your child in each one.

As if that wasn't challenging enough, children are very concrete. As you go through the situations I will present in this book, you will find a problem and a solution identified. But if you are rigid in your presentation of street smarts, your child—who is going to take everything you say somewhat literally—will not have the intuition necessary to figure out what's going on and craft an effective response.

As your child's teacher, you will have to be sensitive to his temperament, cognitive abilities, and decision-making style when you use a street-smarts program. This is a little more complex than it sounds. For instance, your child might be helpful and polite, the kind of child you would feel very comfortable leaving at home alone, even in charge of younger siblings. This helpful, polite child, however, would be at risk on the street when a stranger, intending an abduction, asks for his or her assistance finding a puppy or child. The very trait that will serve him well in one situation could be his undoing in another.

What you want to do is get a fix on the decision-making abilities of your child. Either he has innate street sense or he doesn't. You probably already know what kind of street smarts your child has.

- Is he able to follow instructions?
- In an emergency, where instructions don't apply, could he think on his feet?
- Does he understand cause-and-effect relationships—that his actions, or inactions, have consequences?
- Does he tend to be literal?

Let's look at some personality types and see where problems might exist. If your child has one of these temperaments, you will need to work to overcome them or to figure out compensatory strategies. Keep in mind that the shy four-year-old may well be a social butterfly by second grade. Your challenge is to meet your child where she is through every step of childhood.

THE DAYDREAMER

Getting children to focus can be tricky. The daydreamer, absent-minded genius, or distractible child is going to present even greater challenges because the concept of alertness and vigilance runs counter to who he is. This kind of child probably shouldn't be left in charge of other children, though he can be trained to stay at home alone. Walking home will need special attention because virtually any random occurrence might distract the child. Keep in mind that his temperament is not a justification to keep him in a bubble all of his life. It just means that you will have to train him to focus and to pay attention. This child would benefit enormously from playing the "what if" game (see Chapter 6). I would also post lists of reminders and family rules around the house for him.

THE LONER

Loners present a particular problem in that they attract predators. Any child molester observing a playground scene will gravitate immediately to the child who is alone. For one thing, it is far easier to develop a relationship with one child, rather than two or three. It is also easier to forcibly abduct a single child. But even more important, especially in the area of sexual abuse, is that loners are often lonely. They are easy targets for a warm, attentive adult. They crave attention. A child who is needy in this way is truly at risk. A loner should not be seen alone in public places. He is safer at home alone, and might even be more resourceful than a socially adept child in that environment. He tends to be more rigid in following directions and more devoted to doing things correctly. Obviously, a child with this psychological makeup needs support in cultivating social relationships. But until he has friends, be aware that he is precisely the type of child the predator and child molester seek out.

THE SOCIAL BUTTERFLY

For the most part, a child with a strong personality and social skills is a less desirable victim for predators, but this kind of child is vulnerable insofar as he often will talk to just about anyone. The chatty social butterfly can be so intent on engaging his audience that he doesn't pay attention to the fact that his audience is behaving strangely. The child who is open and friendly should not be discouraged from being so, but he needs to learn to make distinctions. It is hard to induce a kind of wariness in some children; after all, they just want to have fun and enjoy life, and who can blame them? But this gregarious child will usually respond well to clear rules. As long as he has a method for reporting in to you and keeping you abreast of his whereabouts, he should be on the safe side.

MISS PERFECT

The child who behaves perfectly is also more likely to obey someone who does not have her best interest in mind. It is crucial to help this child understand that we do not defer to all adults just because they are adults. True, we want to respect all human beings, but this child needs to know that it is okay to question, disobey, even run away from someone he feels uncomfortable with. Children who are somewhat rigid about manners and doing the right thing can find themselves in dangerous situations just because they want to be polite.

THE FEARFUL CHILD

All children have fears, but some children are more easily frightened than others. With the fearful child, you must address the fears head-on rather than pretend that neither the fears nor the dangers exist. No matter what temperament your child has, the single greatest obstacle to safety is fear. Your child will *always* be safer if he is not scared. When a child is scared, he will figure there is no way out. He will panic or freeze. When a child knows he has choices, even in tough situations, he can respond.

The fearful child may be the most challenging in theory, but in practice he may actually be the most trainable. Half of the battle in teaching street smarts is getting the child to detect danger. Such a child will be quicker to identify dangers (including some that do not exist). Your objective will be to arm him with a set of responses and the confidence he will need to execute them.

TALKING TO YOUR CHILD ABOUT DANGER

Many parents are worried they're going to freak their children out by telling them about sexual abuse, abductions, or other dangers. But you can teach your child all about danger without scaring him. Information does not frighten children if it is delivered in a calm, direct manner.

When you talk to your child about dangerous people or situations, speak in simple language. If, for instance, you are making a point about sexual abusers, you can say, "You know most people are okay, but there are a few people who do bad things and could harm you."

One safety expert, Kenneth Wooden, recommends comparing good and bad people to the weather. The weather rarely ever proves a threat to our existence. But when it does turn bad, we almost always get early warning signals and we take the precautions necessary. People are the same way. We will always get signals from people who are going to be dangerous. We just need to know how to read them and respond appropriately.

Don't give graphic details about abductions or abuse cases. A Roper survey reported that 76 percent of the children interviewed ranked "fear of being kidnapped" as their number one fear. There is no need to give your children fodder for nightmares. But don't pretend kidnappings happen only in the movies, either. If, for example, an abduction occurs in your area and your child asks about it, you can quickly give an explanation and then personalize it: "What would you do if a car pulled up close to *you* while you were walking home from school?" Dwelling on the gory details or trying to employ scare tactics is off the mark, and will distract and preoccupy your child. Your objective is to help your child learn to distinguish between proper and improper behavior by adults. Once a child can identify strange circumstances, he can respond to them intelligently.

Building up his interest in being safe and smart will prepare your child for difficult situations. *Avoiding* the subject of danger will put your child at greatest risk.

SMART CHILDREN MAKE CHOICES

Remember the children who were watching the Coast Guard officer give his lecture while a brush fire was starting up behind him? They said nothing. Once a child sees that something is not quite right, he needs to change the momentum, shift the power, get away, or say no—whether we are talking about a bully on the playground or a camp counselor who seems too attentive.

Most children are very adept at saying no when it comes to eating broccoli or doing homework. But when he is in a strange situation, a child loses his moxie. A polite child especially does not want to offend. A sociable child may not want to risk losing someone's approval or acceptance. A quiet, lonely child may crave affection and be willing to suspend doubt for some warmth and companionship. A very bright child may be curious. All of these children need to know how to say no and get away.

In the chapters that follow you'll learn how to help your child develop the kind of antennae that will alert him to virtually any dangerous situation. But you will need to develop a new mind-set, as well.

Chapter 2

THE LESSON PLAN

Parenting, for the most part, is improvisation. But teaching street smarts requires some planning. You'll need to develop a sense of the material you want to cover and the age that your child will be most receptive to it.

This isn't to suggest that you need an elaborate single-spaced lesson plan like your grade-school teacher used to carry around. But you will need to make safety a priority. It's fairly obvious when to teach a child how to use a spoon or the toilet. But when should you teach that same child what to do if a relative makes her feel uncomfortable? Timing has to do with the situation as much as with the child's developmental abilities.

For instance, one of the first things parents ask me is how old a child should be before he can walk to school alone. Obviously, it would be irresponsible for me to suggest a specific age—say, seven years old—and leave it at that. First, I'd have to know the child. I'd have to see the path he walks to school—is it four blocks or four miles? Is it in the East Village in New York City or in a small town in Nebraska? Are there neighbors along the way or are the streets deserted? Is the child flighty or highly responsible? Obviously, this is a judgment call, one the parent alone can make.

Having said this, I *do* believe that with planning we can approach our children methodically in our effort to teach them to be safe. In this chapter, I'll give you a flexible lesson plan with approximate ages and stages for training your child in basic street smarts, from infancy up to middle school. (See Chapter 8 for specific information on teenagers.) You can select your child's developmental age and read about what he or she should be learning at that point. But don't be rigid about teaching specific tasks at specific ages. None of this is precise. Your precocious three-year-old may be able to internalize more than the next-door neighbor's five-year-old right now. You alone can assess what your child is ready to know and when to introduce it. The ages and stages I've provided are ballpark; I've listed them chronologically so you will see this as an unfolding process, replete with repetition and innovation.

You Can Start on Day One

I admit I am a fanatic about street smarts, but no, you don't have to sing songs about traffic safety to your child in utero. However, you can begin training your child about his body from day one.

It is very important that your child be able to identify

his body parts, even his so-called private parts, by their specific names. The child who can say *vagina* with no self-consciousness is far safer than the child for whom the word is a mystery, possibly one associated with shame. So use the proper names for those body parts, every one of them, from the first day.

In addition, you should be aware that every time you respond to your child's cry of hunger or pain or discomfort, you raise a child who knows he will be heard—and I mean that in a profound psychological sense. Many victims of child abuse are children who are afraid to speak out about the harm they are experiencing for fear of being judged harshly or of not being heard at all. Often they believe they will be rejected or ignored. Your child must always feel safe expressing himself and his feelings, and this perception is built from the earliest days of life.

THE INFANT

In the early months of your child's life you can begin to develop a deep respect and understanding of the dignity and worth of your child. This is more subtle than it sounds. At the infant stage, most babies are treated like dolls or pets, cute little things to be passed around among the neighbors and relatives. There is nothing wrong with getting hugs, but it is important to keep in mind that your child is, after all, a human being! If Grandma wants to hold your baby and your baby doesn't want to be held, honor the child's protests. This doesn't mean that you and your spouse are the only people who can hold him. It simply means you should respect his wish to be touched *or not*. This training is as much for you as it is for the baby.

In fact, stranger anxiety could be viewed as burgeoning street smarts. Knowing someone is different is a piece of important information. It's not a judgment, it's a distinction. As your child moves through this phase and begins to trust again, he will know to establish boundaries based on healthy distinctions.

Meanwhile, infants learning to crawl obviously need their own set of "floor smarts," and you should be meticulous when babyproofing your house. I do not intend this to be a comprehensive discussion of baby safety, but you must survey your home to locate all of its possible dangers to your baby. I recommend that you literally get down on your knees and crawl around to uncover the dangers that exist. Look at bookshelves, electrical outlets, cabinet doors, cords to standing lamps. See what is under the couch and behind the chest of drawers. *Assume that your child will push or pull everything in sight.* Here, as a beginning, is a rudimentary checklist of considerations for the house with a mobile infant:

Living Room

Check for sharp corners on tables, glass tables (for example, what would happen if your child stood up suddenly under the glass?), broken springs popping out of chairs, breakable knickknacks, piles of magazines, pillows that could suffocate, stone fireplaces. Fireplace tools can be dangerous; standing lamps are easily toppled.

BIRTH TO ONE YEAR

From birth to age one, your baby will be a brand-new person every day. Today could be the day he rolls over or begins to crawl. Never make assumptions when it comes to the safety of a newborn.

- Don't give her toys with loose parts.
- Watch her carefully near any body of water—large or small.
- Don't leave her in a playpen with one side down.
- Never leave her unattended on a surface she could roll off.
- Don't tie anything around her neck.
- Say no—let her know you are serious.
- Use proper names for body parts.
- Don't force her to be touched by a friend or relative if she doesn't want contact.
- Use car seats, belt, and buckle properly.
- Babyproof on a regular basis as your child grows and changes.

Another potential hazard lies in household plants, some of which can be toxic if ingested. Large plants can be pulled down by a tug at the trunk.

Windows and doors should have locks.

Bedrooms/Bathrooms

Install electrical outlet covers and cord wraps. Keep vertical blind cords raised (children can choke on them). Store medications in high, unreachable areas (advise houseguests of this practice as well). Keep hot water temperatures adjusted to no higher than 120 degrees. Keep pets and pet foods at bay. Comb the house for small objects children can choke on: coins, buttons, paper clips, tiny pieces of glass, toy parts. When toy manufacturers warn that certain toys are for children over three, what they really mean is that there are small and possibly dangerous removable parts. If your child is three and still explores with his mouth, use common sense and avoid buying toys that might present a risk. Cribs and playpens should meet safety standards, with no hanging toys across the top once your child is pulling up. Safety gates are okay until about the age of two. When your child reaches the age that he can climb out of his playpen and/or crib, reexamine his world and do a second sweep. You must review the house, operating on the assumption that he will at some point be exploring unsupervised. Be careful when you dispose of any plastic bag: children pull them out of the garbage and can suffocate while playing with them. I also recommend installing toilet seat, drawer, and cabinet latches in the bathrooms. If your older child is a wanderer, you might put bells or some other noisemaker on his door so you will know if he's on the prowl. Nightlights are also good to have here and there.

Kitchen

Make sure all lower drawers and cabinets have safety latches on them. Be certain drawers with sharp knives and other blades are locked. Consider a refrigerator lock. When cooking, make sure all pan handles point inward, and never leave a child unattended in the kitchen when something is cooking. Dishwashers can be dangerous for little ones; put a latch on yours. Children like to use the open door as a trampoline, a platform from which to get up on counters, or a food source—as in caustic detergents.

Obviously, the stove is a major concern. Stove-knob covers can be removed and used by you on an as-needed basis. It's a nuisance but worth it for the time being.

Finally, I know that it is wonderful to have your child in an infant seat on the kitchen counter, watching the world and you while you keep busy. But make sure that a sudden movement won't cause the infant seat to slide off the counter. Remember, your child becomes a new person every twenty-four hours—with new strengths and impulses. Monitor your baby closely so you can anticipate any possible mishaps as she grows up, day by day.

Garage/Backyard/Exits

The garage won't be a factor for babies, but it can be an extremely dangerous place for children. Paints, toxic chemicals, and tools all present real dangers to the curious child. The best policy is to get rid of everything you don't need and lock up the rest—especially the chemicals and paints. Make sure you have no unlocked refrigerators or other appliances a child could climb into. Take special precautions about your automatic garage door opener; your child should not be able to activate it, and it also should be gauged to react to even the slightest resistance—for example, your child's head—if accidentally activated.

Home Pools

If you have a pool, you also need to have a pool fence to protect your children and others from entering the area un-supervised. The numbers of drowning accidents and deaths are still staggering; in Florida, California, and Arizona, drowning is still the number one cause of death for children under five. Nationwide it is the number two cause of death in this age category. The troubling fact is that 69 percent of children's drowning deaths occur when one or both parents are supervising their children! Most of the time, parents thought the child was either sleeping or playing somewhere else in the house or yard. Therefore, a pool fence is crucial. Keep all doors leading to the pool area locked at an un-reachable level. Begin training your child to swim as early as you can, stressing safety: find the edge, get to the steps, and *get out*. Review swimming and safety procedures con-stantly (especially during the winter months). Never let other children supervise a toddler in the pool. There are too many distractions.

STREET SMARTS FOR TODDLERS

Once a child starts to move around on his own, he is ready to begin real street-smarts training. It's no matter that his universe might be the lobby in an apartment building or a backyard surrounded by a white picket fence. He is now mobile and there is much to learn.

For toddlers, boundaries are crucial and nothing can be

TODDLERHOOD: ONE TO TWO AND A HALF

This is open season—your child is moving everywhere. Make sure you know how to get his attention in a dangerous situation.

- Always buckle or fasten your child in properly.
- Keep on babyproofing.
- Comb your house for small parts he could choke on.
- Teach him to stay at your side in public places.
- Watch him carefully around bodies of water.
- Teach him to play within your field of vision.
- Teach him proper names for body parts.
- Teach him to pay attention to you when you speak.
- Pay attention to him when he speaks!

ambiguous. In all of your instruction, be specific. If you want to warn your child about a potential danger, don't simply make it off-limits. For instance, many parents will point to a radiator or the top of the stove and say, "Don't touch." At the least, this reveals a very poor understanding of human nature. It is far more effective to say "Hot!," which suggests immediate specific negative consequences.

Your child should develop a sense of danger but not an attitude of fear. Obviously, streets, parking lots, malls—anything outside the confines of the babyproofed home—represent potential danger. A child needs to know to hold your hand, to stay at your side, and not to lean out of the stroller. Yet most children at this age are impetuous and unpredictable. They will run into the street. They will take off in a mall. When safety is concerned you need to get a child's attention—fast. To this end, one street-smart family I know taught their children the meaning of the word *stop* when the children were very young. The parents made up a little stop-and-go game and played it over and over again until the children gained enough self-control to freeze when they heard the word *stop*. Think how valuable that skill might be for a child heading out into a busy parking lot.

So develop a way to get your child's attention. Train him to *listen* to you. I once heard a child psychologist on a morning show who said one of the biggest problems he encountered was that parents couldn't get their children to listen to them. In most cases, the parents had actually trained their children to tune them out. "I tell Johnny a hundred times to take the garbage out, but he just doesn't listen," one parent complained. The child psychologist suggested that the mother had told her child to take out the garbage ninety-nine times too many.

When you are teaching street smarts, you need to be heard—the first time. Your children need to understand that you are serious. At this age, they need to learn to obey your safety-related orders on command, not to mention all the other things you ask of them. Get in the habit of asking your child *just one time* to do everything from putting a toy away to passing his juice cup. If he doesn't respond, *make sure there are consequences*. You are teaching your child to listen and react—one of the most fundamental skills of street smarts.

THREE TO FOUR YEARS

Your child is ready to learn basic concepts of street smarts—from what to do if she gets lost to what constitutes inappropriate touching.

- Teach her her full name, address, and phone number, as well as her parents' full names.
- Start to teach her what to do if she gets separated from you in a public place. Begin to point out uniformed people in shopping malls, store employees with name tags, and so forth.
- Discuss the importance of always asking Mom, Dad, or a caregiver for permission to go somewhere or with someone. Practice this constantly.
- Childproof her room, where she probably will spend more time alone and unsupervised.
- Stress water safety rules, especially if you have a pool in your yard or neighborhood.
- Begin to identify certain body parts—those covered by a swimsuit—as private. Explain appropriate and inappropriate touching.
- Stress the importance of never getting inside someone's car without permission.
- Start the practice of the buddy system.
- Rudiments of fire safety can be taught: stop, drop, and roll.
- Teach her how to dial 911 for help in an emergency.
- Keep communication open: no secrets.

PRESCHOOL SMARTS

Once your child moves into preschool, he will take an enormous leap in learning. Most significantly, he'll be using language. Once a child begins to speak, you will want to start teaching him his name and address; often this can be accomplished in a little song or jingle. He should learn his name, address, phone number (including area code), and parents' names (first and last) as soon as he is able.

He is also capable of learning about his feelings at this stage. If a child can identify his feelings—anger, sorrow, envy, whatever—he will be well on the road to protecting himself from possible abuse. You can begin by making faces and explaining the expressions you make (sad, worried, surprised), or by singing the old favorite "If You're Happy and You Know It," or by looking at books that discuss feelings. Your objective is to help your child put a name to his emotions. Everyone has feelings, and it is okay to talk about them.

The older preschool child also can learn that while he should respect all adults (and children, for that matter), he doesn't necessarily need to *obey* them. This is a tremendously difficult idea to get across, especially when we are trying to encourage our children to be civil and mannerly. The problem is that abusers and abductors count on their little victims to be polite. Adults, by virtue of their size, present themselves as authority figures who should be obeyed. Children need to know that if someone makes them feel uncomfortable, they are not obliged to obey. Indeed, they can run and scream and do whatever it takes to extract themselves from the person or situation without fear or embarrassment.

FOUR TO SEVEN YEARS

These are crucial years for teaching street smarts. Your child is on his own in school or with friends. Make sure you use this stage to establish open communication. Keep the subject of safety foremost in your mind—and in your child's mind.

- Emphasize again the importance of staying with a buddy, especially on field trips.
- Help your child familiarize himself with the neighborhood: safe homes, deserted areas, hidden driveways that could be dangerous.
- Always make your child wear a helmet when riding his bike.
- Tell your child how to identify adults who behave strangely: they ask children for help, they offer them gifts or candy, they stare at them. Explain the remote possibility of abduction and discuss various tricks abductors use.
- Make sure your child knows he does not have to obey all adults. If someone makes him uncomfortable or if he feels danger, he can run away and scream for help. Have him practice a loud scream for help in a low, strong voice.
- Continue discussions about appropriate and inappropriate touching.
- Stress always: no secrets.
- Teach your child that the telephone is not a toy. Establish telephone etiquette and safety procedures.
- Make sure your child is monitored by an adult anytime he is near or at a swimming pool.
- Childproof your house, especially the garage and basement, where toxic materials are stored.

Obviously, you shouldn't interject talk about abusers and abductors in an etiquette lesson; that would confuse the young child. Teach your children that in an emergency, they shouldn't worry about anything but saving themselves. Let your children know that if anyone, even another child, makes them feel uncomfortable, it *is* an emergency and that the most important thing to do is to run away and get help. As you steadily build the child's sense of self-worth and dignity, he will know that no one has a right to violate him.

The preschool age is also the time to begin teaching your child about techniques for survival in public places, from getting lost at the mall (what should she do if she gets separated from you?) to the importance of telling you anytime she intends to go somewhere (can I run next door to the neighbors?). Most of the time the preschool child will be in your orbit, but on the off chance that he strays, he needs to know what to do. When you shop, point out who the cashiers and security guards are. At the zoo, make it clear who is safe: a uniformed guide or volunteer with a zoo name tag. Point out information booths in public places.

Finally, you should also be delivering simple, clear information about fire, car, and home safety to your child at this point. Many four-year-olds have saved the lives of siblings and parents just by knowing to dial 911 in an emergency. You may want to preprogram your phone with an emergency number so that a child has to know only one digit.

TUNING IN TO THE ELEMENTARY SCHOOL CHILD

Once your child is school age, he is capable of absorbing enormous amounts of information. The foundations you laid in the earliest years—identifying body parts properly, learning to express and be comfortable with feelings, having a sense of dignity and worth, knowing to trust instincts, feeling empowered to say no to an adult in an uncomfortable situation, knowing that it is okay to ask for help, being able to listen and stay alert—all of these underlying abilities ultimately are what leads to strong, street-smart children. It should be clear by now that street smarts isn't commando training. It's learning how to be safe in an unpredictable world.

First and foremost, at this stage, is the rule of safety in numbers: your child should learn always to travel with a buddy or in a group. He should be cautioned against playing in deserted areas. You should make him familiar with his neighborhood and he should know where safe homes are. Talk to him about abduction in a matter-of-fact manner— as an extremely rare occurrence that by and large can be avoided. Doing so will make him cautious, but not fearful. This is also the time to make your child aware that it is not necessarily strangers, but people who *behave strangely*, who are dangerous. If you get one point only from this book, I hope it will be that in the vast majority of abduction and abuse situations, the perpetrator is *not* a stranger. Your child should understand that if a person that they know, even a "friend" or relative, behaves strangely, they need to run and get help.

SEVEN TO TEN YEARS

Once a child is seven, she has entered the age of reason and can make important distinctions. These years are for fine-tuning many of the concepts you introduced previously.

- If a child is walking to school, make sure she is with a buddy.
- Continue discussions about abduction and abuse. Answer questions. Explain simply and matter-of-factly. Always emphasize: no secrets.
- Make sure your child continues the practice of asking for permission to go somewhere, and understands that she is never to get into a car without specific permission from her parents.
- Teach your child where to meet you should you get separated in a public place.
- If your child rides her bike, make sure she is conversant with safety practices and wears a helmet.
- If your child stays home alone, make sure she doesn't answer the door or the phone, unless she has determined that the call is for her.
- Review fire safety in the home.
- Coordinate home discussions about sexuality and substance abuse with the school program. Address the "facts of life" in an age-appropriate manner.

Children at this age often answer the door and the telephone. They should be well briefed in this matter. If they are home alone, they should never answer the door. An an-

swering machine should be used, and they should be instructed not to pick up the phone unless they are sure it is a
parent or caregiver on the line. Once a child has left the
confines of home—via on-line or by answering the phone
or opening the front door—he needs to know what the possibilities are and what you expect of him.

Some simple safety education takes place in school during the elementary years, and your job will be to expand
upon and repeat what is taught. At this age, the "what-if"
game (see Chapter 6) will have particular benefit, along
with even more concrete forms of role playing, especially
for fire safety and abuse/abduction issues.

You must stay abreast of your school programs to educate
kids about drugs and alcohol, sex, and child abuse. Generally, schools will introduce the programs to parents first,
and this is an excellent chance for you not only to acquaint
yourself with what your child will be learning in school but
also to brush up on your own street smarts. In addition, in
kindergarten and/or first grade, schools often take children
on field trips to police and fire stations. Foster relationships
with members of both departments. You never know when
you will need the help of one of these men or women, and
you and your child will feel even more secure if you know
who the rescue team is in your area.

The lion's share of what your child learns about street
smarts will come to him during these elementary school
years, when he is intellectually ready and still receptive to
the practical wisdom you have to share with him. Don't
miss this wonderful teaching opportunity.

MIDDLE SCHOOL SMARTS

By the time your child reaches middle school you will in many ways have lost your audience. Though your child is still speaking to you, he is probably not really listening to everything you say, or at the least, he is beginning to question it. In middle school, peers become a greater influence than parents, and your child will not exactly be taking notes when you attempt to lecture him. To that end, you should be aware of who your child's friends are, their parents' names, and their addresses and phone numbers.

TEN TO THIRTEEN YEARS

Your street-smarts teaching days are basically over. Reinforce what your child already knows. If he does not exhibit good safety judgment, be certain there are immediate and significant consequences.

- Keep conversations going about drugs, alcohol, and sex.
- Maintain a list of your child's friends' names and addresses and their parents' names.
- Know your child's school and recreation schedule in detail.
- Continue to talk to your child about abductors and abusers, explaining the lures commonly used on middle school students.
- Keep communication open with your child.

During these fairly crazed years, the most important thing is to set firm, enforceable rules with your children, whether it is about being home alone, spending time at friends' houses, or going to the arcade. Your child must inform you before he or she goes anywhere, even on the most insignificant outing. He should never get into someone's car without your permission.

You may not be seeing eye to eye about everything, but remember, fundamentally, that your child at this age is still a kid. He is a prime target of sick adults and even other children. Stay in touch with him and his feelings, and keep communication lines open.

You Can Never Be Too Street Smart

I stress to parents that there is no such thing as being too practical or having too much common sense. If you can grasp the importance of training your child to be realistic and strong, you will have taken an important first step in fulfilling your responsibility as a parent or caregiver. After all, reading, writing, and arithmetic are important, but they also are essentially meaningless if your child isn't safe or can't take care of himself.

Chapter 3

PEDOPHILES AMONG US

A few years ago I was speaking to a group of parents about sexual abuse. I told them about a photographer who routinely shot group pictures of soccer teams. The photographer had established a reputation for being warm and engaging with children, and he received a lot of assignments from the YMCA and schools. The boys especially loved him. He would always horse around and take extra shots, not just the typical team lineups. One time he had the boys pose with their jerseys off and tossed over their shoulders, sort of the "macho locker-room look," as he put it. Some of the parents were watching and one father found it weird. The father wasn't paranoid or overprotective by nature, but he reported it to the police.

As it turned out, the father's instincts were right on the money. The photographer had a police record for child molestation. He was also a child pornographer. He was superimposing the locker-room shots onto nude photos and selling them over the Internet. Pictures of every child on that team had been bought, sold, and traded by pedophiles.

When I finished telling the story to the parent group, they all shook their heads in disbelief. "I can see that happening in Chicago, Detective Bentz," one woman finally volunteered. "But it's hard to imagine this happening in our neighborhood. It's so . . . perverted."

I agreed that it was perverted; I had seen the photographs firsthand. The photographer had been working right down the street from where I was giving my talk.

All of which brings me to a crucial point: Denial is the most common response to child molesters. The "only in Chicago" attitude is naive at best. But fear of sexual abuse is so overwhelming that many parents respond by looking the other way, as if denying the existence of danger will somehow make the world a safer place.

Obviously, such a response pleases child molesters. In a sense, they count on it. This compounds the problem of child molestation in this country. Most parents will not face the gruesome reality that child molestation and abuse happens every day, in many forms, right in your neighborhood. The U.S. Department of Justice estimates that there are 4 million sex offenders in the United States. In the past decade, reported cases of sexual abuse increased by 2,000 percent. There are a lot of statistics floating about, but studies now seem to agree that one in four girls and one in seven boys under the age of eighteen have been victims of sexual abuse. About 12 percent of all females have experienced a rape, and in 65 percent of the cases, it occurred when the woman was a child. Rape is mainly a crime against children. Pretending it doesn't happen is almost a crime itself.

BODY TALK

The first and most important thing to do in talking about sexual abuse with your child is to get over any embarrassment you might have about the topic. Child molesters agree that a child who is naive about sexuality is easier prey. From birth on, you must talk with your child about his body naturally and freely.

Don't give genitals pet names. Identify the body parts accurately and specifically so your child feels he can be honest about certain parts of his body. You can practice with your child when he is learning the body parts. He should be able to say *penis* as easily as *shoulder, elbow,* or *hand.*

Some parents have asked me about being nude in front of their own children. This is a very subjective decision. I know in Europe, where people have a more relaxed sense of their bodies, parents are often less inhibited around their own children. But I think that sometimes the sight of parents' bodies can scare or put off children, especially at certain sensitive stages of the child's development. In my opinion, you should allow the child to feel confident and strong about his body, clothed or unclothed, and leave your body out of the equation. This, of course, is a personal decision you might want to discuss with your pediatrician.

Finally, emphasize that your child has a basic right to his or her body. He or she owns it. No one else in the whole world has any right to force any kind of unwelcome touching.

THE DEVIL YOU KNOW

Not only do we all have to get our heads out of the sand, but we have to face a terrible fact. Most cases of molestation are perpetrated by someone the family or the child knows.

This means that when it comes to sexual abuse, the idea of "stranger danger" is seriously misleading. In 90 percent of the cases, the sexual abuser is someone the victim knows. Nine out of ten rapes of children under twelve are committed by someone the victim knows. More than half of all sexual abuse is incestuous—that is, committed by a family member.

Obviously, this makes the task of protecting your child much more complex. Strangers are easy to identify. A stranger is someone you don't know. When children think of strangers, they picture frightening characters. In fact, hundreds of children have been interviewed to determine what image comes up when they hear the word *stranger*. Nine times out of ten, the child envisions a tall man with dark hair, often wearing a mustache.

But the person who is most likely to commit sexual abuse against your child is a family friend, a coach, a camp counselor, a member of the clergy, a teacher, a babysitter, or a blood relation. These people do not carry a warning label. They do not look dangerous or creepy. In fact, when I asked one sexual molester what kind of people would commit such a crime, he looked at me straight in the eye and said simply, "Your own best friend."

GOOD GUYS, BAD GUYS

It is extremely difficult to teach a child that someone in their close circle of friends and family might be a "bad guy." You don't want to create constant mistrust, but you do want your child to be able to identify bad behavior. One teacher at an elementary school suggested that children take out two pieces of paper. On one sheet, they were told to draw a "good guy." On the other, they were to draw a "bad guy."

Without exception, the good guys were smiling and neatly groomed; they had on clean clothes. The bad guys, as you might guess, sported capes, beards, and menacing expressions.

At this point, the teacher began a discussion about appearances. She explained that sometimes people who do bad things smile and wear nice clothes. In other words, you can't always tell if people are bad or good by how they look.

So let's look again at "your own best friend" and the individuals who work with your children. Maybe some of these characteristics will seem familiar. If you know someone who in certain ways fits the profile of a molester, you don't have to be paranoid, but you should be concerned. Every child molester I have ever spoken to agrees that parents are far too quick to trust people with their children.

What is a sexual molester all about? Pedophiles, child molesters, and rapists are emotionally arrested individuals who are looking to dominate and control. More than 90 percent are male. Many were sexually, emotionally, or physically abused as a child. Their need for love and affection becomes twisted, and an inadequacy in their own lives leads them to prey on children. Those who are married are often married to women who are childlike in appearance, passive, and small-breasted. The vast majority use pornography, and often they are attracted to sadomasochistic images. Many are chemically dependent. Some seem cocky and grandiose to the outside world, but they are actually extremely insecure. They have a difficulty expressing their anger, and they are emotionally isolated. The average child molester has sexual contact with children about 70 times before he is caught, and 300 to 350 times in a lifetime. More than two-thirds of all sexual offenders who are released from prison offend again. Intriguingly, they are far from being sexual human beings. Their issue is not sex, but control. The easiest person to control is a child. And more often than not, that person targets someone in his daily life—a grandchild, a stepdaughter, a neighbor, a member of the team, a student in class—to groom and then control by sexual molestation.

The crucial point is that a pedophile is not necessarily a stranger, but he or she is a person who behaves strangely. If we can make that distinction with our children, we can help them avoid the worst kind of abuse. What kinds of behavior should we be looking for? What *is* strange behavior? Here are some warning signs:

- The person pays too much attention to your child, showering him with gifts and attention, trips to the movies, weekend outings.

- If a number of children are present, the person still focuses mainly on your child.
- You notice the person staring at your child.
- The person has excellent skills with children, and has put himself in a position to be in contact with children professionally or on a volunteer basis.
- The person has no children himself, but works with children.
- The person likes to take your child to places alone, and actively discourages others from coming along.
- The person is new in town. Predators, once caught or convicted, move frequently.

I have interviewed a number of child molesters and pedophiles who now are in treatment. It is almost impossible to generalize about pedophiles in terms of class, education, or personality type. A leading business executive in our community abuses a young boy in an adult sponsor–type program. A grandfather abuses his preschool granddaughter while grooming his grandson for abuse. A male "friend of the family" rapes and kills the six-year-old girl he often took for ice cream. A door-to-door salesman befriends a neighborhood child, takes the boy into a wooded area, molests him, and kills him. An eighth-grade gym teacher has his female students sit on the gym floor in such a way that he can look down their loose-fitting tops, and even goes so far as to lay on the floor himself so he can see up their skirts. The head printer for the local newspaper—a scout leader—molests his daughter and his daughter's friend. These are people from all walks of life; no one could have predicted they would be pedophiles or child molesters.

But we do know how they work. Their behavior patterns are well established. In all of my interviews, these convicted molesters told pretty much the same story; only the characters and the settings changed. Once they have identified their potential victims, they methodically wear them down. This was true in case after case after case.

First, they find the right victim. Child molesters are looking for the docile, lonely, or somewhat estranged child. As you can guess, the pedophile has low self-esteem to begin with, and he would never dare prey on a strong, confident, socially adept child. At the playground, he is looking for the child who is off alone, who plays by himself a lot. The child who walks home alone from school interests him. In every case, he will prefer someone shy or uncertain. He especially loves children with good manners, who are respectful of adult authority. More than anything, he doesn't want a fuss or a fight. He wants to wear down his prey and make the child his victim.

When a predator pursues an older child, say, of middle school age, he is looking for someone who is particularly vulnerable to sexual curiosity and confusion. (Unfortunately, almost any middle school child meets this description.) Again, he seeks the child who doesn't have enough to do, who is looking for companionship, who is somewhat out of touch with his peers. Sweet, awkward, and quiet children often fall into this category.

Having identified a victim, the child molester begins the grooming process. Almost all child molesters groom the potential victim. They ingratiate themselves not only with the child but with the child's family. In many cases, the pedophile gets pleasure from the hunt and will patiently pursue his victim for weeks, months, even years. The family realizes that this person is spending an inordinate amount of time with their child, but somehow it seems okay.

Sometimes parents are even grateful. For instance, children of single mothers are often the target because a family friend knows the mother will appreciate the presence of what she thinks is a good male role model. In Dallas, where a priest was convicted of abusing dozens of teenage boys, the parents of the boys said that at the time the abuse was occurring they had no clue. In fact, they thought it was great that their sons were spending so much time in "church-related" activities.

What is more, the child molester is often engaging and "good" with children. He will find employment or do volunteer work in settings where he will come in contact with children on a regular basis. He has a warm personality and seems protective. He gives the children the attention they crave. After trust is established, he will begin to break down barriers. He will start with some form of familiar, personal contact—putting his arm around the child, for example. He will make up games that involve touching or wrestling or tickling. Slowly he accustoms the child to his touch so there is no shock value in contact. He will ply the child with ice cream or toys or videotapes or, in the cases of older children, pornography, drugs, and alcohol. His patience is beyond measure.

Good Touch, Bad Touch

Many school districts throughout the country are now using the "good touch, bad touch" program. I endorse this approach and strongly recommend parents follow up at home whatever is discussed in school. (I also find it superior to the concept of "real love, fake love," which some child safety experts recommend. Most adults don't know the difference between real and fake love. How can young children be expected to grasp the concept?)

But studies have shown that the "good touch, bad touch" concept works because of the fight-or-flight response. Every child will instinctively try to struggle or remove himself from a bad situation. A child may not be able to pinpoint it exactly, but he more often than not will know that sexual contact with an adult is somehow bad.

When the "good touch, bad touch" program is implemented in schools, it generally begins at the kindergarten age. Teachers initiate a group discussion, asking what the children believe "good touch" might be. The students volunteer their ideas, and the class discusses them. Then the teacher asks what the children believe "bad touch" might be, and again, the class discusses their answers. I have found that the children are influenced positively by these discussions, because they arise for the most part from their peers. The children seem to absorb the information more successfully in this atmosphere than if the teacher had simply delivered the information lecture-style.

In general, the teacher will help students protect their private parts—the areas that are covered by a swimsuit. She advises the children that those parts should not be touched unless it is required for medical treatment. I am sad to report that as teachers get to the discussion of private parts, I start getting phone calls from distressed parents whose children have reported inappropriate contact in one form or another.

This is why it is so important to be clear with our children. At age five or thereabouts, teach him that "good touch" is a hug or light kiss that makes him feel happy. Good touch is what happens when the doctor gives you a checkup or when a parent or caregiver gives you a bath. Such touching is good for you. A coach giving a pat on the back, a teacher or principal offering a warm hug, a friend greeting you—all of these things can be good touch.

Bad touch is different. Bad touch makes us feel uneasy and confused. Something seems wrong. Bad touch is when someone touches a child's private parts for nonmedical reasons. (And as soon as a child can wash himself adequately, a parent no longer should need to touch a child's genitals *unless* he or she is inspecting for illness or disease.) Bad touch can come from an adult or from another child. Unfortunately, children can also be molesters and we need to be clear with our children that no one—adult or child—should be allowed to bad touch another.

When our sensitive crimes department talks to classes and determines that the children know the difference between good touch and bad touch, we go one step further and discuss "secret touch." We let them know that if anyone touches them, especially on their private parts, and warns them to keep the touches a secret, they must tell a trusted adult or police officer. We point out that there is a difference between keeping "surprises" to themselves and keeping secrets. Keeping a surprise is okay. Keeping a secret is not.

If a child believes that someone is touching him inappropriately, he should be taught to disengage himself as quickly as possible. He should run away and tell a trusted adult at once. Your children should know that they can tell you anything, no matter what.

Again, the pedophile could be a stepfather, a neighbor, the soccer coach. There will be no dark mustache to tip off your child, only behavior that seems a bit too focused, too attentive, too much.

TRAINING YOUR CHILD

A child will not become street smart about sexual abuse if you are vague or casual about the subject. You need to spell things out for your child. By the age of four or five, every child should know that no one has the right to touch his private parts unless it is a doctor, with Dad or Mom present. Explain that once your child can wash his private parts, even Mom and Dad will not make contact, unless it is to apply medication. Sometimes all it takes is one heart-to-heart and a child will know what to do. I remember Sarah, who attended one of my school talks. She was a lovely child and had announced to me that she was going to be a ballerina. A few months after my talk about good touching and bad touching, I got a letter from her.

Dear Officer Ric, Thank you for coming to our school. After you taught us about bad touching, I told my Daddy no. My Mommy made him leave our house and I feel better. Sarah.

The letter broke my heart, but it also intensified my conviction that much of the sexual abuse in this country is preventable or stoppable. Fewer than 10 percent of all child molestations in this country are reported because children are too embarrassed or threatened to talk with their parents about it. Your child must feel that he can tell you anything. He must know that you respect him and he must also respect himself. A child needs you to be clear about his right to his body. Don't let relatives demand a hug. Don't say, "Give Mommy a kiss." Your child needs to know that he has dignity and worth and that no one has the right to make physical demands on him. In addition, you should discuss the following principles with your child.

- It is not okay for an adult to touch you in any way that makes you feel bad or sad.
- If you are touched in a way that makes you feel bad, *it is not your fault.*
- Anything that makes you feel uncomfortable should be shared with Mom or Dad.

MY BODY, MYSELF

One of the great pleasures of parenting is the affection we give and receive from our children. From the time they are newborns, we hold them and kiss them and tickle them. But we also need to remember to listen to our child when she pulls back from a hug or doesn't want to give Uncle Fred a good-night kiss. Too often we treat our children like pets: "Give Grandmother a hug" or "Come sit in my lap." This kind of command takes away the child's dignity and control. Surely you would never command an adult to do the same thing.

When it comes to being touched, a child should know that he *never* has to obey orders, not even from parents. And we should set good examples by being respectful and articulating our respect.

For instance, if you give your child a bear hug and he recoils, immediately pull back and apologize. Ask: "Would you like me to stop hugging you?" If the child says yes, thank him for being straightforward and for speaking up. Remind him that it is *his* body and that no one, not even you, has the right to make him feel even the least bit uncomfortable.

- If someone is touching you and making you feel uncomfortable, you have the right to say no.
- No secrets, ever!

And here is a key point: It is not only wrong for adults to make sexual advances on children, it is *illegal*. Your child should understand that any sexual contact with a child is against the law.

In my experience, this single piece of information has saved hundreds of children from being victimized. Children are legalistic, and black-and-white distinctions empower them. Children who understand that sexual contact with children is illegal can go to a trusted adult with complete confidence that they are doing the right thing. They will be less prone to keep unseemly behavior secret, as they are often instructed to do. The law is their ultimate protection.

IF YOU HAVE SUSPICIONS

What should you do if you suspect someone has abused your child or intends to do so? How should you approach what is obviously a delicate situation?

• Review your child's behavior. Any changes in behavior are important to note. Has she become withdrawn lately? Is she acting out sexually or rebellious? Have her tastes in clothing changed? Does she show reluctance to be with the suspect? How are her grades? Social relationships?

• Talk to your child about her relationship with the person you suspect. If a child claims to be the victim of a seemingly insignificant crime, listen to him or her. Take the child seriously. Don't ever blame the child for what happened. Emphasize the concept of the law to your child; no one has the right to violate a child's dignity.

SEXUAL BEHAVIOR: WHAT'S NORMAL, WHAT'S NOT

Anytime you suspect your child might be in danger of sexual abuse, you should contact your local law enforcement agency. Granted, I get some hysterical phone calls from mothers afraid of sexual abuse because they found their four-year-old innocently playing with his genitals. But for the most part I would rather hear from citizens than have them wait around "to be sure."

Let me review what is normal behavior, to clear the air here. For example, playing doctor and engaging in bathroom humor are normal, especially if the child, when asked to stop, does so without objection. It is normal for a child to be curious about sexual behavior and ask questions about it.

Flags should go up, however, if your child is interested *only* in sexual topics. Oftentimes, children who are sexually abused masturbate inordinately and are overstimulated; they also feel intense shame and guilt about their behavior. Such children might have been sexually abused or exposed to pornography.

Children who live in highly dysfunctional families or those who have been sexually or emotionally abused will often be sexually active at a young age, and very difficult to treat. In the most extreme cases, children will sexually abuse other children in a coercive manner. They are compulsive about their sexual activities and cannot stop without specialized treatment.

- If you have concerns about a specific person, ask your child what kinds of things they do alone together—where they go, what they watch on television. Start slow and leave the questions open-ended so your child can give you a narrative. Don't put words into your child's mouth or come on too strong. If your child is being molested, he will be terribly uncomfortable talking about it. Undoubtedly, he will have been told to keep it a secret, possibly under the threat that if he tells someone, horrible consequences will follow (harm to parents, denial, shame, and so forth).

Don't go to the suspect and accuse him or her of wrongdoing. Enlist the help of professionals. Contact a counselor at school, a private psychologist, a trusted pediatrician. If a crime has been committed, your operating on your own may muddle the investigation and even destroy chances of a successful prosecution. The law in this area is complex. There is a wealth of support available for families in this situation, and you should not hesitate to seek it.

- Honor your intuitions. Some people have the uncanny ability to sense when someone is too friendly or too aggressive. Pay attention.

- Contact your local police. With the National Computer Registration of Sexual Offenders, they will be able to track down any prior convictions. More than 60 percent of all convicted sex offenders are on parole or probation. Each state has a phone number you can call to get this information. Some local departments, like ours, are setting up books so people can come in and look at the faces of the offenders. Actually, it's good to find out how many convicted molesters you have in your neighborhood. You'll be disturbed and surprised.

NO MEANS NO

Ways to Say No

There is more than one way to say no. In situations where a child is uncomfortable being touched, he could say something like: "Please stop that." Here are some possibilities: "That makes me uncomfortable, please stop touching me like that." "This bothers me." "I don't like this, leave me alone." If the person continues, the child can threaten: "Stop now or I will tell my mother." At that point, he should get a parent or call 911 for help.

It's Okay to Say No

For a child, any odd behavior, especially sexual behavior, can be embarrassing. If your child reports a problem, he needs to know that he can tell you anything that happened without condemnation or judgment. If he is scared that the perpetrator might retaliate, his parents need to know immediately.

If It Feels Bad, Say No

A child also needs to know that anything, even a slight contact that makes him feel uncomfortable, is okay to resist. If an adult does something to make a child feel uncomfortable, whatever it is, it needs to be relayed to a trusted parent or adult. The child must be reassured that no matter what, you will support him and his claim. Explain to the child: "I want to teach you ways to be safe when we're not together. We will talk a lot about being safe and smart, so you will always know what to do."

If your child tells you a family member is touching him inappropriately, listen and tell him you support him completely. Offer your love and understanding. Do not make the child tell the story over and over again. This will frustrate the child, and increase the likelihood he will recant just to avoid the painful experience of repeating it endlessly. Control your emotions, and those of your spouse, if that is a factor. If you suspect sexual abuse, the Department of Human Services Child Protection Unit or a local law enforcement agency will help you immediately. Most police departments have someone specially trained in sensitive crimes and will arrange for a medical examination if necessary. A trained detective will take one statement from the child, which if it is done correctly will be all that is necessary.

For counseling and sources of information, you also can call the Victim Services Hotline (212-577-7777), the National Center for Victims of Crime (703-276-2880), or NOVA, the National Organization for Victim Assistance (202-232-6682).

A FINAL WORD

Human behavior, as we have seen, is predictable. We can predict how a child molester might operate. We can predict how certain children might respond. We also can see how a horrendous crime, like sexual abuse, might alter forever the life of its victims.

I was sexually abused as an eleven-year-old. To give you a clue about how deep this kind of experience gets buried, I hadn't really come to terms with it until I started making notes and doing research for this book, and I am a married man in my forties, the father of two teenage boys. It is no coincidence that I have a big place in my heart for the children I see who are victims of sexual abuse. My experience, being molested by a family friend who took me on a weekend fishing trip, left me questioning myself mercilessly. For years I wondered if I had done anything to provoke or invite this man's advances.

Obviously, I hadn't done a thing. But children never know that, not really. Every time I help a child get through a similar episode, aid him or her in detaching from the extraordinary guilt and shame, I heal. Actually, I am lucky. Instead of becoming a predator myself, I was able to take the healing route and bring good out of a nightmarish experience.

Many children are not as fortunate. The cycle of abuse continues generation after generation, often complicated by other criminal behavior. For this reason, I underline the importance of protecting your children.

Chapter 4

CHILD ABDUCTORS

A mother and her five-year-old son went to an amusement park for a day of fun. It was the child's first visit, and he was having the time of his life. After a while, the boy had to use the rest room. His mother was uncomfortable about letting him go into the men's room on his own, but shrugged it off. After all, what could happen on such a lovely day?

The mother waited outside the door of the men's room for several minutes. Some men and boys came and went, but her son did not emerge. She did notice an adult carrying a sleeping child, but the child was a redhead. She started calling for her son, but he didn't answer. Panicking, she grabbed a male passerby and asked him to go in and check the rest room for her. Her son was not there. Immediately, she notified the park authorities. They closed off the park and checked every child as he exited. An hour of inspections turned up nothing. As she stood at the gate watching each child pass, the mother began to despair. Then, once again, she saw the man carrying the sleeping child with red hair. The child was wearing Sesame Street sneakers, just like her son's. She looked again. It *was* her son.

As it turned out, the abductor had drugged the child when he went into the rest room and dyed his hair red. Were it not for the Sesame Street sneakers, the boy probably would never have been seen again.

A story like this is every parent's nightmare. It is the kind of crime that makes the world seem an impossible place in which to raise children. How can we prevent elaborate schemes like this from happening? This is where every parent *and* child needs to be trained in street smarts.

THE GOOD NEWS

In truth, successful abductions by strangers—people unknown to the child or the child's family—are not as common as we perceive them to be. The Polly Klaas incident in 1993, where a twelve-year-old was kidnapped from her own room, was unusual. Most stranger abductions occur in public places. The National Center for Missing and Exploited Children estimates that approximately 4,500 children are successfully abducted by strangers each year, though that figure might be somewhat inflated. Most researchers agree that there are about 125,000 abduction attempts annually. In the majority of cases, the children are eventually recovered. About 200 to 300 a year are never found or are found dead. And contrary to what most people believe, children aged twelve and older account for the majority of child abductions and murders, with girls twice as likely to be the victims as boys.

Obviously, our goal is that your child will never be among those statistics. The difference between a successful abduction and a foiled attempt is about two to three seconds. Luck and timing are the primary factors, but *prevention* is the key. It takes just a few seconds for a team of abductors to slow down their car and whisk a small child off her bicycle. If the child knows to scream bloody murder and do everything she can to avoid being pulled in the car, she increases her chances of survival tenfold. If she had been riding with a buddy in the first place, the abductors probably would have passed her by; they don't want a potential witness, and it is almost impossible to abduct two children at once. A simple shift in circumstances and your child is no longer a target.

The odds are slim your child will ever come face-to-face with a criminal abductor, so don't impart a sense of paranoia to your child. Your aim is to generate a healthy respect for unusual or dangerous situations. If your child can navigate her world with this attitude, along with some basic street smarts, the odds are literally one in a million that an abductor will succeed in taking your child away.

The other factor in your child's favor is that we now know how abductors operate. They are remarkably predictable. They have a variety of motives—kidnapping, sexual abuse, and random violence—but they have similar modes of operation. For some reason, they are most active

---

SCHOOL DIRECTORIES: A FREEBIE
FOR PEDOPHILES

Our school district eliminated school directories in response to the number of adults who were cruising through the little books in search of victims. Typically, an abductor or sexual offender will gain information about children's names, ages, and phone numbers. He will learn at a glance the child's teacher's name and who his classmates are. The problem is that this kind of information, used in a phone or playground conversation, can completely disarm the intended victim. How could anyone who knows your teacher's name be bad? Be careful about what you print for public consumption, especially when it comes to your children.

---

in March and April. They are most attracted to preadolescent children or young teenagers.

Now that we can anticipate the kinds of tricks they might use, you can discuss them with your child. The more she knows, the smarter she is, the easier you'll sleep.

GAMES ABDUCTORS PLAY

A long-term abductor lacks social skills, which is why he relies on tricks rather than a more spontaneous approach. Being unskilled socially, he is easily put off. In many cases,

COMMUNICATION IS CRUCIAL

One of the most important things you can do is set up a good communication system in your family. But this goes both ways. If we want our children to behave in a certain way, we need to set an example. Our children should let us know where they are, and we should keep them posted as to our whereabouts. If you have dinner plans at a certain restaurant and switch to another at the last minute, call and let your children and/or their caregiver know. If you are going to be late picking them up or coming home, call. If checking in is a way of life, it won't become a power struggle, especially during the teenage years, when it could be perceived as constrictive.

the slightest bit of resistance will stop an abductor in his tracks.

If your child can recognize the games abductors play and respond to them by getting away fast, he likely will never be a kidnapping victim. Here are the classic abductor's lures. The following tricks are often employed by adults who wish to lure children away to kidnap or abuse.

"I Need Your Help"

Sweet, helpful children are susceptible to abductors who can persuade them that they need help: to rescue a puppy, a toddler, a favorite doll. Even in a public setting the abductor can beckon the child to an isolated corner. Obviously, you want your children to be helpful, kind human beings.

But you need to explain that it doesn't make sense for an adult to ask a child for help, whether it is for directions (a common ploy) or to find the thousand dollars someone left in the shrubs. (Children like cash. This is another frequently used approach.) When a child asks an adult for help, it's not dangerous. But when an adult asks a child for help, something is not quite right. This "I need your help" trick is popular among criminal abductors because it works.

"You Ought to Be in Pictures"

Abductors who are interested in sexual contact often ply children with flattery. There are thousands of documented cases of children being lured to "modeling" studios, groomed, and then assaulted. Many predators will pretend to be modeling and acting scouts, and young girls in particular are extremely vulnerable to the flattering notion that they could be a model or in films. Warn your children. Tell them about this lure, and make it clear to them that any reputable photographer or scout would contact parents first. Tell your children never, ever to pose for a stranger. If someone at the park or in a shopping mall asks to take a picture, a child should *get away*.

"You're in Trouble"

Another approach used by abductors is the bad child trick. The abductor, often with a phony ID or uniform, will go up to a child and tell him he has done something wrong and has to come with him. The crime the child is accused of could be anything: a playground violation, shoplifting at a mall, or running a bill at a restaurant. Regardless of how far-fetched the accusation is, an authority figure can lure a child into his vehicle on this basis with extraordinary ease. Again, a child needs to know instinctively never to go with a strange person and never to get in a strange vehicle. *Children should know that they have every right to question an adult, even a "police officer."* In reality, a police officer would never arrest a young child. If a police officer wants to approach an underage child, he generally goes to the child's school or contacts the parents. If a teenager is in a shopping mall or restaurant and a uniformed "police officer" accuses him of a patently false crime, the teenager should question the person, ask to see his credentials, and turn for help and support from the nearest security guard, cashier, or other store employee. A child should be wary and always trust his instincts. This ploy is used less often because most child molesters know it is a felony to impersonate a police officer, and they won't be able to talk themselves out of a case if they're wearing a police badge.

"I Know Your Parents"

In this instance, the abductor pretends to have come at the request of the child's parents to take the child home early. The abductor might say: "Your parents asked me to rush over and pick you up. What's your name? I need to know if you are the right child." The child, off guard because of the urgency, reveals personal information "confirming" that she is the "right" child. A savvy abductor can do a quick interview with the child and learn her parents' names, her family password, and where she lives in a matter of minutes. Once all seems legitimate, the abductor can lure the child to his vehicle.

"Come with Me or I'll Shoot You"

It's hard not to respond to a physical threat. Occasionally, an abductor will intimidate a child by telling her to get in the car or be killed. Or he'll threaten to kill the child's parents if she doesn't get in a car. If your child is confronted with a weapon, he should run and scream as loud as he can. A criminal does not want to get caught, and if a child is yelling, the criminal is most likely to respond by driving off. This is a crucial point for children. Explain to your child that it is illegal to make a threat. If an adult does so, the child should *get away*.

PREVENTING ABDUCTION IN THE FIRST PLACE

The best way to deal with the fear of abduction is to instill some habits that serve to prevent it from happening in the first place. Reviewing the common tricks identified above with your child is one way. But the more you keep your child out of danger in the first place, the better the odds are that the unthinkable will never happen.

Parents often ask me: how old does Jack need to be before I let him go with his friends to the mall? When can I leave him at the library to do his research alone? I can never give the answer in actual years. It is always a judgment call, but it doesn't have to be entirely subjective. Remember the little boy who was abducted from the rest room at the amusement park? How old should a child be before he goes to a public rest room alone? There are numerous issues here. Always start with the basics: Can he remove his

RECOGNIZING A CHILD IN TROUBLE

Teachers, doctors, and social workers are all trained to spot children who might be living in some form of captivity. But what if you suspect a child is in trouble? Every situation is different, but there are some patterns we have seen in the past two decades. Abducted children often live with a single male "parent" posing as an uncle, father, or grandfather. The "parent" may seem overprotective. The child may not have a memory of his early childhood and may mix up dates, times, and places. The child may seem wary of law enforcement agencies, authority figures, and his or her "parent." Poor performance in school is also a marker. If you do suspect that something is not quite right, speak to someone: a school counselor, a police officer, a social worker, a teacher. Don't hold back information for fear of being a busybody. You may be the only chance that child has.

clothing and dress himself again, if necessary? Are his zipping and snapping skills adequate? A child should not be left on his own if he must require help from strangers.

Then, too, does he have the dexterity to latch and unlatch stall doors? What would he do if a stranger struck up a conversation? How would he react? Have you trained him to run and yell if any stranger makes him feel uncomfortable?

These are the kinds of questions we need to ask ourselves before we loosen the apron strings. We don't need to obsess. We just need to consider a child's readiness, just as we did when he first learned to walk.

Meanwhile, here are some basic practices for you to follow:

• *Identify your children*. Daily, make a mental note of what your child is wearing. If you are going to a crowded public place, dress your child in a bright, easy-to-see color. You can keep an eye on an orange T-shirt much easier than on a white one.

Make sure your children have proper identification. Even your baby should have some form of ID. I would suggest writing the child's name, address, and phone number on a little piece of paper placed in her shoe, or in permanent marker inside the shoe itself. This works well for children until they are old enough to remember their name, address, and phone number—about four years old for most children. Children must know this information. Children also should know their parents' first and last names.

In addition, many school districts now offer identification programs where children are fingerprinted. If you take advantage of these programs, be certain to explain this activity in a way that does not create paranoia in your child. Dr. Benjamin Spock believed that the fingerprinting process was unnecessarily frightening to children, and voiced a concern that we were raising a generation of children who would not trust. To me, it is a matter of communicating with our children in a reassuring way. I would recommend that you initiate a discussion with your children. Do not try to fingerprint your child yourself. Several companies sell home-fingerprinting kits, but unless you are trained, the impression you will come up with will be

FAMILY ABDUCTIONS

The vast majority of abductions are not enacted by strangers, per se, but by family members, usually in a custody fight. A lot of people discount these abductions, figuring that if a child is with a family member, it couldn't be all that bad. But at least one out of four (about 75,000) of these abductions by family members result in physical, sexual, or emotional abuse of the child. Anyway, think about it: what kind of person would kidnap his own child? In a majority of the cases, researchers identified the motive in family abductions as "anger or to cause pain." It is the rare abduction that is an act of love.

If you fear that an estranged spouse or other family member might be contemplating an abduction, the targeted child is in a precarious position. If the adult is angry or depressed or otherwise imbalanced, be sure you have a custody order, even if it's temporary. Your attorney should be aware that the custody arrangements could be violated. The language should be very precise, (with exact times and dates), and should be communicated to everyone with whom your children spends time. Don't just file it in with the release card in the school office; let each of your children's teachers know about it, as well as their coaches, piano teacher, tennis instructor, babysitters, and so on. Let everyone in your child's life know about the potential problem with the estranged individual. To the extent that you can, be sure your child is never alone, at home or on the street.

If the individual is especially menacing and threatens to take the children, document the threats and file them with the family court.

worthless. It is better to rely on your school or a local law enforcement agency.

I am not a major proponent of dental IDs—placing serial numbers on children's teeth for identification in the event of an abduction or a murder—although some of my brethren in police forces around the country support them. I think it's excessive, and that spending the same time and effort educating your child to be street smart in the first place is a much better investment. But I do recommend that you keep current records of your child with vital statistics such as height, weight, hair or eye color, and any identifying birthmarks. Have a current photograph on hand, as well. (The National Center for Missing and Exploited Children recommends you update this every four months during heavy growth periods.)

Businesses in your local area will be able to help. Blockbuster Video designates one month a year to allow parents to make free videotapes of their children. Polaroid has created more than five million KidCare identification kits, distributed and underwritten by companies such as Toys "R" Us, Sears, Home Depot, and Kmart.

If you have a disabled child, your local law enforcement agency should know about him or her, along with any information that might be relevant.

• *Never leave your children unattended.* This seems so obvious. Yet every year children are abducted from parked cars. If you have to run into the grocery store for milk, drag your children with you. Do not leave them in the car. If your eleven-year-old wants to stay in the car and you feel comfortable with that, make sure he knows never to open the door for anyone, not even someone the child knows, and that if he senses danger, to honk the horn until help comes. But wouldn't it be easier and safer just to have the child go into the store with you? He might feel put upon, but at least he'll be safe.

Inside, make sure your child stays at your side. In what is probably the best-publicized abduction case in this country—the slaying of five-year-old Adam Walsh in Florida—his mother allowed him to wander in a department store for just a minute or two, just yards from where she was shopping. Children should not be roaming around public places alone, even if the place is your neighborhood supermarket. Also, do not leave children unattended in the shopping cart.

- *Decide on a place to meet if you get separated.* This is just as important for adults, especially in foreign travel situations, as it is for children in the local pharmacy.

- *Don't judge by appearances.* The "stranger" stereotype—dark and ominous in appearance—doesn't necessarily apply to an abductor. Your child should know that an abductor can look clean and friendly. He might even be the cheerful neighbor who lives down the street.

- *Ask before you go anywhere.* Even through the teenage years, a child should have to ask before he or she goes anywhere. I realize that teenagers are more likely to *announce* where they are going rather than ask, but the important point here is that they are trained to share their whereabouts with an adult and to avoid impetuous decisions and spur-of-the-moment schemes. A child from an early age should know that his parents need to know exactly where he is at all times.

- *Use the buddy system.* Abductors go for their victims one at a time. If your child is with a buddy, the whole process becomes too much of a hassle for the abductor. On the other hand, don't be lulled into thinking that just because your child is not alone, he is safe. Sex offenders are drawn to places where children hang out, such as shopping malls, restaurants, movie theaters, playgrounds, and parks. In these circumstances, a child might go off on his own for any number of reasons. Train him to take a friend, even to the rest room. Being with a buddy isn't a 100 percent guarantee of safety, but it's the best first step.

- *Don't put children's names on their possessions.* Once a child hears his name, a huge barrier has been broken down. A lunch box, bracelet, backpack, article of clothing, pencil box—anything that bears little Johnny's name is a freebie for a predator. If you are marking your child's possessions, put the name inside of the items, so they can't be viewed by predators at a distance.

- *Use a family code word.* It is a good idea to have a family code word, known only to family members. I can name a dozen instances where a would-be victim saved her- or himself by demanding a code word from a would-be predator. In New York, for example, an eleven-year-old girl was waiting for her mother to pick her up in front of the local swimming club. A man she didn't know pulled up and told her there had been a fire at her home and that he had been sent to get her right away. The child asked the man for

WHAT TO DO IF YOUR CHILD IS
ABDUCTED BY A FAMILY MEMBER

If you know who the abductor is, you can assist in the work to locate your child. First, obtain legal custody (if you have not already) along with warrants. Then distribute posters of your child as far and wide as you can.

You can also check:

- the abductor's bank to see if there has been action on the account
- credit card companies
- the post office for forwarded mail requests
- the pediatrician to see if records were requested or sent
- the abductor's employer (was last paycheck forwarded?)
- car rental companies
- airlines
- traveler's check companies
- your child's school—notify them to make you aware of any requests for records

the family code word. The abductor knew he had been foiled, wheeled his car around, and jetted out of the parking lot. Unfortunately, he was never found. By using her family's code word, the child probably saved her own life.

The code word works when an abductor uses the "emergency" ploy. It is especially effective when the perpetrator is someone known to a child—a neighbor or family friend, even a family member. In numerous cases of sexual abuse I have worked on, the parent of a child's friend has come to pick up a child from school, soccer practice, or the park, intending to take the child to either groom or abuse him. The family code word has often stopped the molester from getting to square one.

The family code word isn't perfect. Many times, abductors who are aware of the device will trick the child. They will rush up, acting as though there is an enormous emergency, and ask the child for the family code word. The child, anxious and off guard, blurts it out, and then the perpetrator acts as though the child must indeed be the right one, having identified his code word correctly. You can imagine how confusing and tricky this could get. Further, if a child needs to ask for a code word, *he should do it in the presence of another trusted adult.* This is extremely important. Otherwise, a criminal might get frustrated and yank the child into his or her car. Despite these complications, it behooves the family to have a code word. Make it simple: a pet's name, favorite athlete, favorite television show or food. And admonish your child never ever to tell anyone what it is.

• *Stay alert when you are out in public.* Your older child should be discouraged from wearing headphones on public transportation or while jogging. All children should know—and be reminded—to stay away from cars. *If a car pulls up to ask for directions or help, run away.* Take off in the opposite direction. Always remember: It doesn't make sense for an adult to ask a child for help.

• *Don't depend on fancy safety gadgets.* With millions of parents concerned for their children's safety, manufacturers have come up with numerous safety devices to deliver peace of mind. But they can't always deliver a safe child. When a mother bought her only child a yellow beeper alarm, she breathed a sigh of relief. She had trained her little daughter that if someone tried to hurt her, she should pull the pin and a siren would go off. One day, while walking three blocks to a friend's house, the child was approached by a strange man. She activated the siren. The alarm fell to the ground and the man dragged her into a nearby house. When two neighbors heard the alarm, they wrapped it in duct tape to get rid of the annoying sound. Eight days later, they found the girl's battered body in a back alley. If the child had been taught to flee from a predator, instead of relying on the alarm, she might be here today.

IF A CHILD IS ABDUCTED

Abductions are rare, but 125,000 are attempted every year in this country. Many programs have been developed to teach children what to do in the event of an abduction. While I emphasize training that helps a child avoid the abduction in the first place, prevention doesn't always work. It can be frightening to discuss this with a child, but believe me, your fear will be greater than that of the child. If you are calm and direct, you can share some important points with your child.

YELLING FOR HELP

One of the key components for any child who is fleeing danger is to yell. But most of us have raised our children not to yell. If your child is in danger, you don't want him to use his "inside voice." You also don't want him to yell like a child whooping and hollering on the playground. You want him to yell for help in a deep, strong voice. Girls especially need to know that a high-pitched, two-second "ah" isn't going to get anyone's attention. The yell must be low and as long as the child can hold it. Teach your child to take a deep breath and to yell "Help me!" or "Fire!" Practice with him. If a child yells in the midst of an abduction, he will totally change the dynamics of the situation. He will throw off his abductor momentarily and gain a sense of empowerment. Something as simple as a good strong scream could save your child's life.

Here are a few:

- If you are in a public place and someone approaches you and makes you feel uneasy, get away. Run, don't walk, from people who make you nervous.
- Never ever get in a car—especially a van. Do whatever you can to break away, even if the abductor has a gun. Once you are in the car, it will be much harder to escape.
- If you are near a phone, dial 911 (it's free) and say, "I've been kidnapped." You don't need to put in a

coin for the phone to engage. Once you've called, don't hang up. Just let the phone dangle.
- Look for someone to help you.
- Try to get attention. In a public place, yell. Rip your shirt. Throw something out of the car.
- Don't try to fight back. Flee, don't fight. A child's impulse to use karate or boxing against an adult predator is misguided and dangerous.

WHAT TO DO IF YOUR CHILD IS MISSING

Your ten-year-old walks from school, and is always home by 4:15 P.M. It's 4:45 P.M. What should you do?

If your child is missing, most likely there is a plausible reason for it—a communication problem, a caregiver's mix-up—and he or she will be recovered quickly. *Don't panic.* This is easier said than done, but it's crucial.

First, search the house or the immediate area where your child was last seen. Don't spend more than a couple of minutes on this. If the child was last seen at home, look in every possible hiding place, beginning with under the bed or in the dryer. You would be amazed where I have found children.

Call anyone who might be aware of your child's whereabouts. Be efficient. If you cannot find your child, contact the police at once, as seconds count. Have a current photo of your child available and, if possible, a list of the child's friends and their phone numbers and addresses. Have a list of the places the child could be. You will be asked for a physical description (including identifying marks), a description of the clothing your child was wearing when he or she was last seen, and where the child was last seen. Have someone wait at home by the phone to keep it open for important calls.

If the child has been abducted, the first forty-eight hours are the most important to recover the child alive. If my child was abducted, I would not rely only on the efforts of the police. I would gather friends, family members, and neighbors and ask everyone to get the word out, especially to people in high places. I would have my team go door-to-door at first, looking for someone who might have seen my child. I would call every radio station and television network and the local newspaper. I would alert everyone to the fact that the life expectancy of a criminally abducted child is no more than forty-eight hours.

I would also be wary about people I didn't know who came to the rescue. A lot of phony services and private investigators come out of the woodwork when there is a crisis involving someone as precious as a child. Check out every organization and service with the National Center for Missing and Exploited Children. Have a levelheaded friend or family member with you to help you sort out who's who.

Your police force will probably enlist the help of missing persons operations nationwide if the child is not found after a cursory search. Request that your child be listed in the National Crime Information Center Missing Persons File.

Call the National Center for Missing and Exploited Children at 1-800-843-5678 or 1-703-235-3900.

If the suspect is a family member, you might call for information from the Child Find mediation program, at 1-800-A-WAY-OUT.

Chapter 5

HOME ALONE

It's small wonder *Home Alone* was a big hit. For children, the fear of being alone is basic; even adults can feel uneasy in certain circumstances. The phone ringing in an empty house can bring chills. A creaking noise, a barking dog, a knock on the door—all can trigger fear. But today, in unprecedented numbers, American children are home alone. With a majority of families two-income, about 45 percent of all American children between the ages of six and thirteen are latchkey children—children who are regularly left at home unsupervised for some portion of the day. While in my opinion leaving even a mature six-year-old at home alone is ill advised, at some point, with good training, most children can manage it and even be in charge of younger siblings.

In this chapter, we will take a look at some off-the-street smarts. We will evaluate your child's readiness to be home alone and discuss how to prepare your child for self-care. As with most street-smart issues, chronological age is much less a factor than developmental age, along with the ability to think clearly and quickly. We can determine if *your* child is ready to be left home alone—whether it is for a quick fifteen minutes while you run to the store or for an entire day while you are at work.

Let's start with the basics. This may sound obvious, but have you asked your child how he or she feels about it? Some children will seem ready on the outside, but on the inside, they are terrified. Even if there is bravado at the surface, dig a little. Talk it over. Listen carefully. *Don't force the issue*. Also remember that there is more to being ready than knowing how to dial 911. A child must know how to entertain himself, combat boredom, take care of his siblings (if that is part of the deal), and be at peace in an empty house.

I realize that many parents work and have to make arrangements for their children. If your child is not ready, try to find a neighbor or friend to watch over him after school. Ease the child into self-care bit by bit. Bear in mind also that children are works in progress. One day they might be fine at home alone; the next day, fears will arise. For instance, in preadolescence, many young girls develop random fears. A ten-year-old girl might have handled being at home alone easily, but at age twelve, the same girl might be overwhelmed with anxiety. Staying in touch with your child is *crucial*, especially if you are a working parent who depends on your child's ability to handle time on her own.

ARE YOU OVERPROTECTIVE?

Many parents err on the side of laxity when it comes to keeping their children safe, but some parents are actually *over*protective, creating a different set of risks for their child. You might recognize it in yourself: you're the one who won't let your child drink from a drinking fountain at school for fear of germs, you apply sunscreen to your child hourly (no matter that it's winter), you can't let your child out of your sight even for a second without complete and total panic. In manageable doses, of course, all of these concerns are valid. But if you are constantly hovering anxiously about your child, you are creating enormous anxiety in him or her. Often, overprotective parents have experienced a jarring loss or difficult pregnancy. Other overprotective parents were all but ignored during their own childhoods, and they compensate. In any case, it is important to note that if you are overly protective and cultivate anxiety rather than street smarts, your child will be at risk whenever an out-of-the-ordinary situation develops. Your child will be the most defenseless among all children because his fears will be greater and his resourcefulness far short of what he'll need, since Mom and Dad always "did" for him. Keeping children perfectly safe is not an achievable goal. Your child will skin his knees and get his feelings hurt and occasionally even get lost. But he will also heal and find his way home, if he has the street smarts to do it.

GETTING STARTED

When it comes to establishing at-home independence for your children, it pays to go slowly and methodically. One street-smart parent I know used a basic weaning process to introduce her child to being on his own. First, she would go to the neighbors for ten minutes, after rehearsing some basics with the child. Ten minutes, over time, turned into thirty minutes, then an hour, and so on. These practice sessions allowed the child to work out many of his fears and concerns and helped him prepare to be home alone. Instead of going over a huge list of survival skills in one shot, the mother was able to discuss and review different issues over time. It was a brilliant approach.

Once you have determined that your child truly feels comfortable on his own at home, take a hard look at the situation in which you are leaving your child. Consider the environment, inside and outside. Start with this checklist:

- Locks on doors: Are they adequate? Can your child open them easily?
- Keys: Have you left them under the flowerpot or on the sill, where predators and burglars look first? Is the key tagged with your child's name or address on it? (Wrong, for obvious reasons.)
- Can you see who is at the front door without them seeing you? A peephole or window that gives a child (and you) a vantage point on the front door is important.

- Lighting: At night, your yard should be illuminated. Inside, there should also be enough lights on to suggest lots of activity—as opposed to the presence of one lone child.
- Are there overgrown bushes in which someone could hide? Ladders lying around that someone could use to get to your second floor?
- Do you have an answering machine? (Every home with children should have one.) Just as you baby-proofed your house for your toddler, you must "proof" your home from every angle before you leave your child to his own self-care.

Neighbors are vital players in the life of a latchkey child. If your neighborhood block has houses designated as safe havens, make a point to get to know those families and introduce your child to them.

Your next move as a street-smart parent is to increase the margins for safety by establishing some guidelines. For example, when your child comes home alone he should have a ritual for entering the house. He should always have his key out and ready. Once he is safely inside, he should engage the security system, if you have one.

Most children who have the ability to reason and conceptualize can handle the following rules. Post a list like this one—with your own unique additions—near the family telephone or in some highly visible location. (Obviously, if your child cannot read the guidelines he is too young to be left on his own.)

LESSENING THE GUILT

Many parents of latchkey children spend more time worrying about their children than training them. Business analysts have even coined the phrase "three o'clock syndrome"—that period when they tend to see more mistakes and restlessness among employees whose children are just leaving school for an empty house.

The moment your child gets home, he should be trained to lock the door and call you to let you know he is home. Both of you will benefit from that phone call, and if your child wants to call again, don't discourage it. Instruct your child what to do if for some reason you are not reachable by phone.

Have a snack ready for your child. Discourage cooking unless you have an older child (though teenagers are often more careless than well-trained ten-year-olds). Candles, lighters, fireplaces, and so forth are off-limits.

Consider getting a pet if you don't have one.

Have open conversations about your child's fears. (Ask him what frightens him most and don't cut him off by assuring him that he is too old for such worries.) If your child has numerous nightmares or is depressed or has elaborate hiding places, he might be wrestling with fears.

Keep your child informed as to your whereabouts, especially if you are going to be late.

Arrange for a neighbor or adult friend to be on hand when your child needs someone to turn to immediately in an emergency or even with a minor concern. Have a special get-together with this person to make your child feel comfortable about contacting them. Show the surrogate how seriously you take his or her role and how appreciative you are with thoughtful small gifts or notes from time to time.

Home Alone Rules

1. Do not answer the door.
2. Use the answering machine. If the call is for you, you can answer it. If it is for your parent or sibling, let the machine take a message.
3. Do not use the stove or other high-risk appliances. (Be specific.)
4. Stay inside.
5. In case of emergency, call Mom or Dad or 911 (or equivalent emergency number).

I suspect that a skilled seven-year-old could handle the instructions above, but all children are different and most of us do not know how our children might respond to a crisis—since only in rare circumstances has our child ever been put to the test. What's more, the basic rules above are mostly don'ts. A street-smart child must also *react* and be *proactive*. We say, "Don't answer the door," but what if it is a person in a police officer's uniform (a common ruse for abductors)? We say "stay inside," but what if the family pet is loose and in danger of being hit by a car? What if someone keeps calling and leaving disturbing messages on the machine? What if you came home and discovered you didn't have your house key? It is in dealing with the various what-ifs that we can truly see if our child is ready. We can use the what-ifs to train our child as well. (See Chapter 6 for sample questions.) Remember, danger and risk are always the exception in life, not the rule, and what we want to see is how our children will react to the exception.

In general, the home-based emergencies will fall into these categories: fire, bad weather, burglary, injury, illness, and accidents. Let's see how we can prepare your child for each situation.

FIRE

Fire safety is one area that schools and local fire departments address adequately, especially in the preschool and elementary years. But again we face the problem of truly *training* our children. The majority of children are exposed to only one or two lectures or presentations. You must make sure your child has internalized the information.

Here are some suggestions for the whole family:

- Have routine fire drills. A child should know that if he smells smoke or if the smoke alarm goes off, he should leave the house immediately and call the fire department from a neighbor's phone.
- Review exit paths from every room and make certain you have an escape ladder (available at most hardware stores). The kitchen should have a fire ex-

tinguisher. (Don't store it above the stove, since it would be inaccessible in the event of a stove fire.) Smoke alarms should be checked periodically. Children should know what a smoke alarm sounds like so they can react.

- Make sure your child knows how to dial the fire department and give his name and address.
- If the house is on fire, children should have a meeting place outside of the home to make sure everyone is present, safe, and accounted for. When a local boy's house began to fill with smoke, he knew what to do: he met his family at the big oak tree. That simple direction and the boy's ability to follow it meant safety.
- If a child's clothing is on fire, he or she probably has been taught to stop, drop, and roll. Review this with your child periodically. Remind him, in case of fire, not to open any door that is hot to the touch. Leave a smoky room on hands and knees.
- Before you leave a child, make sure no combustible materials (pot holders, towels, curtains, newspapers) are near the stove. All electrical appliances should be unplugged (irons and hair dryers, in particular).

Remember, if your children have a family plan of action, their chances of survival in almost any situation are high. Conversely, if a child isn't trained, his or her chances of handling an emergency are pretty low. A few years ago six-year-old twins, Michael and Nicole, who had not been trained in street smarts, faced a crisis they could not handle. Their mother had just left when smoke began to fill

PERSONAL FAMILY PHONE BOOK

Ever since our children were young, my wife, Pam, and I have kept a personal family phone book. It includes emergency numbers and the names and addresses of all of our doctors, dentists, and everyone who worked on the house, from the plumber to the electrician. We also have a page for each of our son's best friends, especially those with whom they spend a lot of time. (In this way, if one of our children was missing, we could make calls to all of their friends efficiently and calmly, to rule out an innocent explanation for their absence.)

I would recommend you get a three-ring binder and put together a similar directory for your own family, for babysitters, and in case of an emergency, especially if your child spends time at home alone. Walk him through the book and talk to him about who you included and why.

their apartment. Nicole went to her room and lay on her bed. Michael hid under the kitchen table. Their instincts were totally wrong. Nicole died. Miraculously, Michael was rescued. If only they had left their apartment, they would be together today.

BAD WEATHER

Bad weather can be more manageable than other disasters in that you occasionally have some lead time. Most bad weather comes with a warning, and if it is really serious, a parent can either come home or make arrangements to have the child moved to a neighbor's house for safety. But every year thousands of children in the United States face severe weather conditions with no adult supervision. If bad weather comes up suddenly or if for some reason a parent is unavailable, a child needs to know where to go and what to do, whether it is an ice storm, a tornado, an earthquake, a hurricane, or an electrical storm.

This takes some research and planning. If your area has dramatic swings in weather—say, you live on the West Coast, where earthquakes are a possibility—then your task is going to be far more complicated than that of someone who lives in a milder zone. In all cases of disaster, children should be taught to save themselves first and *never* try to recover or preserve material belongings. Children should know to stay inside, turn off the television, and stay in a place away from windows or doors. (For tornadoes, choose a spot in the basement, or if there is no basement, in a bathroom or closet where the child should remain.) In less dangerous situations, the primary concern is power outages. Often phone lines are down and parents cannot get through to their children, or all electricity goes out. Have flashlights (with extra batteries), a water supply, and a battery-operated radio in a special place. Instruct your child never to light candles during a blackout because of the increased chance of a fire developing.

The key to training your child for bad weather is preparation and repetition. Once or twice a year, have a practice drill to see if your child has the street smarts he'll need in times of natural disaster.

BURGLARY

No parent can bear the thought of his child face-to-face with a burglar. And though burglaries do occur when children are home alone, the possibilities are very remote if your house is properly secured. Most police departments will inspect your home at no charge and give you ideas about making the place more secure.

A security system is expensive but can go a long way in bringing safety and peace of mind. But whether you have one or not, you should always keep your windows and doors locked. Never place a key in a mailbox or under a flowerpot. Do not put your name or address on keys. Do not let your child wear his key on a chain around his neck. Be circumspect about giving keys to household or yard workers unless you have known them for a long time. Keep landscaping trimmed so burglars do not have places to hide. Don't leave ladders lying around.

Obviously, the risks of dealing with a break-in are greater for a latchkey child in that he generally comes home from school to a presumably empty house. If anything looks amiss—for instance, a door is ajar or a window open—a child should be taught to run to a neighbor's immediately. The child should never enter the house. He should call the police and his parents and wait.

If a child is at home alone and hears an intruder enter, he should get out of the house if possible. If he can't, he should attempt to call the police immediately and then hide in a closet or a bathroom with the door locked until the police arrive.

FIRST-AID KIT

Every home should have a first-aid kit or cabinet where first-aid medicines and bandages are kept. In addition, children should be taught how to apply a bandage and what kind of ointment to use for cuts, along with other basics.

If your child is home alone often, you might want to get her her own first-aid kit. Here's what you might include:

Bandages
Hydrogen peroxide
Cotton balls
Antibacterial ointment
Tape and dressings
Ice pack
Ipecac (to induce vomiting)
Thermometer
Calamine lotion for insect bites
One child's dose of an aspirin substitute

ACCIDENTS, INJURY, AND ILLNESS

Over 20,000 people die in home accidents every year, and more than 2 million require medical attention. Obviously, this is an area of serious concern, but you don't have to train your child to be a paramedic in order to leave her home alone. Again, good prevention measures will eliminate the lion's share of problems and dangerous possibilities.

Some simple steps like these will go a long way:

- Lock firearms up and out of sight.
- Make the swimming pool off-limits without adults.
- Pick up toys and debris so people don't trip and fall.
- Lock up poisons and medicines that could be toxic for children.
- Forbid cooking unless a child is very well trained in using specific appliances.
- Require the child to stay inside. This is difficult, but it eliminates insect bites and stings, dog bites, and a host of accidents.

Meanwhile, children occasionally get sick and hurt themselves. A street-smart child is trained in rudimentary first aid. My wife, Pam, is a nurse, and teaching our sons first-aid basics came as second nature to her. But anyone can teach the basics and, interestingly, children are eager for concrete practical information. Here are some general guidelines provided by Dr. Stephen Lazoritz, head of pediatrics at Children's Hospital of Wisconsin.

A cut or wound: Show your child how to wash cuts with soap or clean them out with peroxide and apply a simple dressing or bandage. For wounds that bleed excessively, a child should be taught how to apply direct pressure for approximately five minutes to arrest the bleeding. You can practice on your child and have your child practice on you.

Insect bites or stings: If your child is allergic to bees, I would be very cautious about allowing him to play outside when an adult was not on the premises, unless he knows how to administer his own treatment (generally, a shot). Otherwise insect bites and stings can be treated by scraping the stinger out of the wound (if possible) and applying an ice pack.

Animal bites: With animal bites, it is important to wash the wound well and cover it with bandages. An adult should be notified immediately. If the bite is from an unknown dog, it has to be reported to the local humane society, and serious bites should be reported to the doctor.

Nosebleed: Children get nosebleeds frequently, and they can be scary. A child should know not to lie down but to sit up. It would be smart to go to the kitchen or a bathroom if it is a major nosebleed (so as not to drip blood all over the house). Press the bleeding nostril to the center of the nose and continue to apply pressure for about five minutes. If the bleeding hasn't stopped, press the nostrils together for another five minutes. If after ten minutes in all you are still bleeding, call the doctor immediately.

Something in your eye: If you get dust or dirt in your eye, don't rub. Blink your eye a few times to see if you can clear it. If you are unable to clear it, get adult help. If a liquid chemical—such as a cleaning fluid—has gotten in your eye, wash your eye under the water faucet for at least fifteen minutes. Cool or lukewarm water feels best. An adult should take you to the doctor just to make sure no damage to the eye has occurred. If the eye burns, you should go to the doctor or the emergency room *immediately* for help.

HIRING A BABYSITTER

If you have determined that your child is not ready to be at home alone or in charge of siblings, your task is to select competent child care. The American Academy of Pediatrics urges parents not to hire babysitters who are younger than thirteen. If you do use a teenage sitter, it is your responsibility to train the person or to make certain they are trained. The American Red Cross babysitter training course and programs like Safe Sitter (317-355-4888) are a good start. Check references. Interview her or have her come over for a short paid trial, while you are on the premises. Don't be afraid to ask her what she might do in certain emergency situations. Leave adequate emergency numbers (police, fire, pediatrician, dentist, ambulance, and poison control). Write out the names and ages of your children and any allergies they may suffer. Obviously, leave a number where you can be reached. Ask the sitter to come at least fifteen minutes early so you can acclimate her to your children and your home.

Poison: All poisons should be locked up or put out of reach, but sometimes children do ingest them. The number of poison control should be prominently placed near the phone, and a child calling should know what was ingested and the approximate amount. Ipecac should be kept on hand in case poison control suggests it be used to induce vomiting.

Burns: Forget the butter, that's an old wives' tale. Burns should be chilled. Have the child hold the burned area under cold running water. Serious burns should be reported to an adult immediately as the wounds may be prone to dangerous infection.

Broken bones: It's difficult even for physicians to determine if a bone is broken without the use of X rays. If a child suspects he has broken a bone, he should get adult assistance immediately.

Choking: I am not going to cover cardiopulmonary resuscitation (CPR) in this book because, I really believe it is something that needs to be demonstrated rather than read about. Your local hospital, American Red Cross, or American Heart Association will have information on where to take a course in CPR, which will cover a host of emergency situations. Meanwhile, you can do a lot to prevent a choking accident by teaching your child the following:

- Cut your food into small pieces.
- Don't run with food in your mouth.
- Don't eat while lying down.
- If you are using a Styrofoam cup, don't bite off pieces of the cup.
- Do not put pieces of jewelry in your mouth.
- Do not put anything in your mouth that is not edible.

Your child should know what choking is, especially if he is in charge of a small child who is prone to such an accident. (For instance, a baby would not be a candidate for the Heimlich maneuver, because it could crush the baby's ribs.)

SAFE HOME CHECKLIST

Here is a list of items that will help to keep your home safe. Be sure you have all of the following on hand and in good working condition:

- Flashlights
- Fire extinguishers
- Smoke alarms
- Chain fire-escape ladder for second floor
- Telephone answering machine
- Good outside lighting
- Window of break-resistant safety glass or peephole so visitors at front door can be identified
- An intercom system
- Security system, if possible
- Good secure locks on windows and doors

DISTURBING PHONE CALLS

When a child is at home alone, strange phone calls are deeply disturbing. This is why I strongly advise having an answering machine. With an answering machine, the child does not have to make contact with the outside world unless she wants to. If the call is from a parent, family member, or friend, the child can pick up. If not, the machine answers and no one knows the child is home alone. Another option is to get an unlisted phone number.

I am concerned when families use their children to record answering machine messages. They can be cute, but they can also be just what a predator wants to hear. When you record a message, have an adult do the talking. If you are a single woman, consider having a male record a tape for you. Don't use first names. "Susie, Joe, and Clara aren't here right now" tells me Clara is an only child. I can call her back and ask for her by name, which is a disarming and effective first step for a predator. Instead of first names, use the phone number alone ("this is 555-2726") or reference the family's surname. That should be more than enough information for the legitimate caller.

If an annoying phone call is placed to your home, push any button and say, "Operator, this is the call," and watch how fast the person hangs up. It's an old trick, but it works, especially on your children's friends, who often are the culprits. If you do have repeated problems with crank calls and caller ID is affordable in your area, it might be worth the investment. Do not be shy about reporting any truly unusual phone calls. Obviously, you are not going to call in law enforcement for calls of the "your refrigerator is running" or "Prince Albert in the can" variety. But if a caller threatens bodily harm or makes any kind of troubling statement, hang up and call the police immediately.

Chapter 6

THE "WHAT IF" GAME

The "what if" game could save your child's life. That might sound like an overstatement, but when you see how it's played, you'll probably agree. Virtually any child who can communicate can play. You can play the game anywhere. It works with any number of players. There are no losers, because everybody who plays learns vitally important information.

I encourage you to play the "what if" game once a week with your child. One mother told me she played the game every Monday, on the way to her daughter's ballet class. Another made it a routine to play it on her car-pool day, and the whole car pool benefited. If you can get in a routine, that's optimal. If you can't, just play the game every time you think about it: while dinner is cooking, while you're waiting in line at the movie, while you're hanging around the pool. Even one round could make a real difference.

The "what if" game is essentially a forum for discussion about safety and an exploration of key decisions a child might have to make in his life. To help you get started I have assembled a series of questions organized by categories: home, school, public places, and the family. In each case, the questions I have posed come from real-life situations I've dealt with, where a child has made the wrong response and suffered terrible consequences.

As you play the game, resist the temptation to fill in the answers for your child. Don't rush the child or guide him until he has had time to respond. As you review the questions, you will see it doesn't take much imagination to see where the wrong decision could lead.

Of course, answers will vary from family to family, and there can be many solutions for one problem. The important point is that you help the child walk through the steps of decision-making, thus preparing him well for a crisis or uncomfortable situation should it occur. Keep in mind that the questions presented here are just samples to get you going. When you play the game, don't stop with the first answer. Probe the situation. For instance, you ask your child: "What if you are at the shopping mall and find yourself alone?" A street-smart child would know to look for a person in uniform, such as a security guard or police officer, and to ask that person for assistance. But what if no such person was in sight? The child might then go to the person manning the nearest booth, a ticket taker or cashier. If the clerk asks for the child's name and address, the child would be able to recite it, because a street-smart child knows all of his vital information. This conversation might also lead to the idea of establishing a meeting place "in case anyone gets lost" when family or friends go to public places.

Remember, it doesn't matter if your child gets the answer wrong or reveals flawed decision-making. If this happens, lead him to the right answer in a simple, straightforward way. Actually, you almost want your child to answer incorrectly. If he does, you'll be able to address the issue in a casual, nonthreatening environment.

Once you get a feel for what we are doing here, you'll be able to improvise without limit.

Let's look at some typical questions and explore together the way you might choose to answer them.

HOME

You are at home and the telephone rings.
- What if you were home alone, with no adult present?
- What if the caller asks where your parents are?
- What if they ask for your first name?
- What if they know your first name, but you don't know them?
- What if they ask for your last name?
- What if they ask you for your address?
- What if they tell you that they are your dad's boss?
- What if they say they are the police and they need to know your name?
- What if they tell you they are from the fire department?
- What if they tell you it is an emergency?
- What if they tell you they are from the gas, electric, or telephone company?
- What if they tell you that your family won a prize,

and they just need the name and address to send it to?

- What if they say they will hurt you or your parents if you don't tell them?

In general, predators use the telephone to gain information and establish a connection. By identifying themselves as some kind of authority—the police, firefighters—they are able to get children to volunteer information they would not offer otherwise. If anyone identifies himself as a policeman, your child should ask him for his direct line and call him back, even if the "authority" insists it is an emergency and there is no time. The same holds true for a utility representative or a hospital worker in the emergency room. All of these people in an emergency situation would be reachable at a verifiable phone number. Anyway, when was the last time you were called by the police or fire department or a utility company? It's never happened at our house.

Naturally, if an adult is home, the phone call should be turned over to him or her straightaway.

If your child is occasionally home alone, an answering machine is crucial. It eliminates the need for the child to respond to crank callers or predators. They can be instructed to answer the phone only if they know who the caller is. If you don't have an answering machine, you might set up a code so the child will know if you are calling. I know some parents who will ring twice and hang up, and then call back, which works quite well.

In addition, caller ID is a good feature for recording calls and identifying callers.

Someone knocks on the door.
- What if the person is wearing a police uniform?
- What if the person is wearing a delivery uniform (for example, UPS, Federal Express) and says he needs a signature or he cannot leave an important package?
- What if the person says he used to live in your house and just wants to take a quick peek around for old time's sake?
- What if the person says an emergency has happened and they need to use the phone?
- What if your mom is taking a shower?

First, if an adult is home, only an adult should answer the door. This might seem extreme, but it is the safest way for a family to operate. I recommend a peephole or a protective glass window in doors, or some vantage point where you can see who's at the door—whether you are an adult or a child.

In general, if a child is home alone, I tell him or her not to answer the door under any circumstances. A few years ago, in a peaceful Texas town, an eight-year-old girl was kidnapped and murdered. She was a careful, well-trained child—so well trained, in fact, that in one instance, when she was home alone, a police officer came to the door and she refused to open it. Her parents had told her never to answer the door, even if it was an adult in uniform, and the girl showed excellent judgment. But about a month later, when a neighbor came to the door—a friend of the family's and an ex–police officer—the child let him in. The neighbor told her there was a terrible accident and that the girl's parents were in the hospital. He said he would take the child to the hospital. The girl, fearing for her parents' lives, opened the door and accompanied the neighbor. The neighbor had a gambling addiction and owed thousands of dollars. He threw the child into the trunk of his car and drove three hundred miles away to orchestrate a ransom scheme. Ultimately, his scheme didn't work, and he brutally murdered the child.

I know that some parents have a list posted next to the door of people who may come in—family members, neighbors, or friends. This might present an option, but I would be prudent about whose name got on the list.

What if you heard strange noises . . .
- in the front yard?
- on the second floor?
- at a window?
- at a door?

What if you smelled smoke?

Any indication of fire should provoke in a child a set response. If you smell smoke, you call loudly and tell an adult immediately, while exiting the building. Children should not be responsible for saving others, they should be responsible for saving themselves. They then should dial 911 at a neighbor's. A child should know what to do if he sees smoke, sees fire, and so on, as each requires a different response (see pages 84-86). Again, this is one area that requires more than a single conversation or an isolated drill. You should review various fire scenarios repeatedly to make certain your child knows what to do.

SCHOOL

What if you are at school and . . .
- Someone comes up to you on the playground and he or she doesn't work at your school?
- A school employee wants to take you into a private room?
- A school employee wants to take you somewhere off campus?

In school, there are two kinds of people: children and authority figures. Children are trained to respect and obey all authority figures at school, and that is as it should be. But when a school employee does not have a child's best in-terests at heart, the child needs to be able to detect that and respond to it. This means you are going to have to have some difficult conversations, especially for children, upon whom most subtlety is lost.

If a child sees an adult on the playground who is not a staff member, this should be reported. Generally, visitors are required to check in at the office of most schools, though in practice, this rarely happens. Still, it is far more prudent for children to report the sight of a stranger than for everyone to assume he or she is someone who has a reason for being there.

A child should know that it is not proper for a school employee—teacher, custodian, coach, anyone—to take him off campus. But what about the coach in his private office? What about the custodian in the boiler room? A child can be pressed into odd situations with little effort. If he is going off with a school employee to anywhere private, the child should be trained to at least let another school employee know where he is going and with whom and for what reason. The child should be trained to tell his parents, as well.

- What if someone offers to give you a ride to school?
- What if the bus driver gets sick on your way home and you have to get off the bus?
- What if someone calls the school and tells you that one of your parents is ill or has been injured and that you are to leave with that person right away?

One of the key points I would like readers of this book to be most vigilant about is preventing their children from getting into a car—any transportation, for that matter—without their parents' permission. If a child is walking to school and is offered a ride by a neighbor, the answer is no. The answer is no because a child's parents need to know where he is at all times and they are assuming he is walking to school. Since they are not there to ask for permission, the answer is simply no. The answer to the bus question, a reverse situation, is the same. Never get off the bus. If your parent believes you are there, you are to stay there until your parent is contacted for further instructions.

If someone should call with a reported emergency and tell a child (and the school office) he or she is to go with her, the answer is no—unless the person is an authorized driver. Many schools require parents to list the names of the people their children are permitted to ride with. If that person is on the list, fine. Otherwise, again, the answer is no.

- What if you are with your teacher and he or she touches you in a way that makes you feel uncomfortable?
- What if you are with your principal and he or she touches you in a way that makes you feel uncomfortable?

By now, you know what the child needs to do in the situations outlined above. Review these questions and see where it takes you and your child conversationally. The fact that you have discussed these situations with your child shows him you are accessible and nonjudgmental and that, heaven forbid, if anything like this ever did happen to him, he would be prepared.

PUBLIC PLACES

What if you are at a public place (playground, library, mall) and . . .
- An adult asks you to look for his lost kitten or puppy or child?
- An adult tells you that there has been an emergency and that he has to take you home right away?

- An adult comes up to you and wants to play?
- An adult or teenager wants to take pictures of you?
- Someone offers you a ride home?
- Someone offers you a treat—candy or ice cream, something tasty?
- Someone you don't know calls you by name?

Most of the scenarios described above are early scenes from an abduction. We now know that there are a handful of tricks that seem to work quite well with children. The stranger who appeals to a child for help is the most popular and successful. Other ploys include flattery, treats, and telling children that their parent, friend, or other close family member is in a crisis and needs them. Remember, it makes sense for a child to ask an adult for help, but not the other way around.

The last scenario—what if someone calls you by name?—could lead into an excellent discussion about strangers. We want our children to know that all strangers are not dangerous, though a few are, and that all of the people we know are not safe, though most are. This discussion is probably the most important one you can have on a repeated basis with your child. If someone calls you by name, he could have learned your name by seeing your lunch box or hearing a friend call for you. That doesn't mean you should feel comfortable with this person. How would your child react? What would he think or do? How would he know what to do?

What if you are in a public place without supervision and . . .

- You notice an adult taking pictures of you?
- An adult seems to be following you?
- An adult follows you into a public rest room?

If a child is not under the supervision of an adult, he has to make split decisions about everything from what's for dinner to whom he can trust. I put in the question about the adult taking pictures because we had a pedophile who used to do that at a water park in pursuit of an armpit fetish. Children were oblivious to the fact that a strange man was shooting rolls of pictures of them, and ultimately these children ended up in pornography circulated to pedophiles. Children should be cautioned not to pose for photographs, especially for people they don't know.

Meanwhile, if they sense they are being followed, children need to seek the help of an adult immediately. If they are followed into a public rest room, they should get out. If they are followed by a car down the street, they should remember always to walk in the middle of the sidewalk (not too near the curb, as abductors in cars present the greatest threat), and never to run down an alley or a shadowy walkway. They need to run to safety, whether it is the home of a friend, a library, a gas station, or a bank. This is another instance where it is crucial that children have a trusted adult to turn to—someone they actually know or a person in uniform (police officer, security guard, or company employee).

As a general rule, children should pass strangers who are walking on the sidewalk toward them at a safe distance—at least three feet. They should cross the street rapidly if for some reason the stranger makes them uncomfortable. If a stranger intends to take the child's possessions, the child should immediately relinquish whatever it is the person wants, and then run. Under no circumstances, even under the threat of death, should a child get into a car with a stranger. Once a child is trapped in a car, chances are that he'll not get out alive.

What if an adult is driving you—a parent or a friend of the family or a friend's parent—and he or she seems extremely tired or drunk?

Children should know that it is dangerous to get into a car with someone who has been drinking or doing drugs, and that they are under no obligation to obey the adult or humor him by getting in the car. Babysitters who find themselves in this situation should have some line like "I don't feel well. I'd really like my mother to pick me up"— anything that can buy them an out. During the middle school years children are constantly on the go, and parents must chauffeur them each way. If your child suspects that an adult is not sober, he should not get in a car with him.

What if someone in your family . . .
- Touches you or kisses you in a way that makes you feel embarrassed or uncomfortable?
- Tells you not to tell anyone about a present that they bought for you?
- Asks you not to tell anyone about something you did together?

- Is babysitting you and gives you a bath and touches you in a private area where you normally wash yourself?

We have covered many of these scenarios in earlier chapters, but by asking your children these questions and discussing the answers, you will always come back to the importance of your children knowing that they own their bodies, and that no one has the right to touch them inappropriately and that they should never keep secrets from their parents. If the children in this country could absorb these two points, we could arrest the epidemic of sexual abuse. Unfortunately, there is no magic spell. The only way we can do it is with education, one child at a time. Start with your family.

Chapter 7

KIDS IN CYBERSPACE

Every day I patrol the Internet just the way other under-
cover officers patrol the streets. In minutes, posing as a
young child, I can attract known pedophiles in the area
(our police unit has an arrangement with various Internet
access systems that allows us to track the behavior of convicted or suspected criminals). I routinely monitor their
activity on-line in various chat rooms.

I cannot tell you how easy it is for a prospective victim—a child—to be identified and located on the Internet by adults who intend harm. For criminals looking for
lonely, bored children, the Internet is tailor-made. Many
reclusive, shy children find the computer world a sanctu-
ary. Even worse, the thrill of the hunt for pedophiles adds
to the excitement of the crime. The Internet is a playground, where these molesters can pick and choose their
victims without even being seen. Their goal is to get a
face-to-face meeting, and they are willing to go to great
lengths and apply enormous patience to get their victim.
They are willing to "groom" their prey over months, even

years, with caring conversation (they are great listeners), promises of gifts (often computer games and hardware), and sometimes even drugs, alcohol, or sexually explicit materials. For a lonely middle school or high school student, or an elementary-age latchkey child, the lure may be irresistible.

Another factor for both the predator and the child is that the Internet is the ultimate fantasy world. Children like to pretend to be someone they're not on the Internet, and there's no one to stop them. Brunettes will pretend they are blondes. Girls will pretend they are boys. Twelve-year-olds pretend they are seventeen-year-olds. When they are in cyberspace, children are more straightforward, explicit, and aggressive. This fantasy atmosphere makes them far more reckless than they would be in real life.

For example, my co-author, Christine Allison, has a teenage daughter who has been versed in safety issues. Her daughter is fun-loving but levelheaded, and a first-rate student. While Ms. Allison and I were working on the book here in Wisconsin, we attempted to communicate with her daughter on-line and in disguise. Using the computer as a resource, as pedophiles do, I was able to find out the name of the local private boys' school, locations of shopping malls around town, clubs, and favorite hangout spots. With this insider information—or at least enough to bluff my way through—I chatted with her daughter for hours pretending to be a cool local guy. Her daughter fell for it hook, line, and sinker. No harm was done. No danger existed. But that same guy could have used the chat as the first of many conversations, leading to a face-to-face meeting. Or harassment. Or worse.

In other words, the computer is a stage. The technological age has created a whole world of actresses and actors. It is difficult for children to understand where fantasy ends and reality begins, which plays beautifully into predators' hands. In truth, there is no crime or real danger in just chatting on the Internet as long as a child keeps personal information to himself. Ms. Allison's daughter didn't reveal anything about herself, but she did fall for the con. A less wary child might have been lulled into revealing personal information.

Not only is the Internet a fantasyland, it is hypnotic. The on-line live chat medium has hooked tens of thousands of children. The moment they are bored or don't know what to do, they head for the computer. Children online lack perspective. Hours pass, and they don't know it. When a child loses a sense of reality, he also loses whatever judgment he has.

Of course, none of this would matter if your child were merely working at a computer in your family room. But he's not just in your family room. He's on the Internet. This is crucial for parents to keep in mind: the Internet is a *place*. When your child is on-line, he is in essentially lawless territory, and fair game to anyone who comes along. America Online, which is probably the most popular service among children, has minimal staff supervising the chat rooms. And wherever there is poor supervision, you can bet there will be troublemakers.

Not only are your children vulnerable to pedophiles and pornography, but the Internet is filled with hate literature and graphic violence. I have encountered numerous circumstances where children have been "stalked" on the Internet by people who have bullied them and harassed them with obscene messages. Some children have been pursued by creepy lovesick characters who refuse to leave them alone. Though millions of children use it, the Internet is not a toy. Your child needs limits. Once you get an idea of what's out there, you will be better able to set limits that make sense.

GET COMPUTER SMART

For me, the most disturbing aspect of kids surfing without supervision on-line is that many parents have no clue about computers. Wake up, people! This is like letting your child go off with a group of strangers to a place you have never heard of. In virtually every case I have dealt with, the parents were completely out of the Internet loop.

If you are computer illiterate, consider taking a crash course at your local library or high school. Or have your child give you a tutorial. You even could make that part of the deal: If your child wants to use the computer, he needs to teach you how it's done. Have him show you his favorite chat rooms, his buddy list, his favorite places to surf. His technical smarts may be light-years ahead of yours, but you still have him beat on judgment.

PUT THE COMPUTER IN A
PUBLIC PLACE

One of the smartest things parents can do is to keep the computer out of the child's bedroom. From a safety standpoint, it is far preferable to have your computer in a common room in the home, rather than off in a private corner. My sons are twenty and eighteen, and even so, I insist that our computer be in full view in our workout room. If I ever wonder what's up, I just hop on the treadmill.

And that's another thing. When your children are on the computer, walk in, patrol, pull up a chair, make your presence felt. If your teenager was having a party, you'd look in every now and then, just so the attendees "know" to behave. The same goes for the computer.

Another important step: Make sure it's clear that it is the *family* computer, not your child's computer. Never should he have the sense that the computer is his own private world where no one else dare venture. What's more, stay in the vicinity of the computer when your child is online. Your child should have the sense that you could show up any minute. Many schools have instituted this practice in their computer rooms by having Internet chaperones, basically parents whose very presence—roaming the rows of terminals—discourages students from heading into places they shouldn't.

A final control parents can have over the use of the

Internet is to establish a set time of day and length of time a child can be on-line. Any variations on this schedule would have to be cleared with the parent, reminding the child that the use of the computer is a monitored privilege, not an unconditional right.

Beyond that, there are some basics that could protect your child from serious danger. I recommend that you begin with these simple rules, and even that you post them on a sheet near the computer terminal. As you go along, you might add more.

The first rule: *Never give out your real name, address, or phone number on the Internet or your personal identification code.* Most users access the Internet with a password so they can surf without revealing their real names. It is easy to entrap children who "forget" and give out their name. In addition, *never* send a picture of yourself to someone on the Internet. It could be used to create pornography or to identify you on a school playground.

The second rule: *Never ever agree to a face-to-face meeting with someone you met on the Internet unless you are accompanied by a trusted adult.* Furthermore, *if someone asks to meet you face-to-face, tell an adult immediately.* One of the most common ploys is for an Internet-savvy pedophile to pretend he lives in another state. In truth, he lives in the same town. After he has groomed his victim, he pretends he has a business trip or sports tournament that is going to take him through the victim's town. What a wonderful coincidence. Since this may be the "only chance they'll ever have to meet," he proposes they meet at a local hangout, whether it is a hotel or a McDonald's. He applies just enough pressure to make the victim feel guilty if he doesn't show up for this "chance in a lifetime" meeting. He also tells the victim not to tell anyone; it should be a secret.

As long as your child has not released any personal information, he would be safe from the predator I just described. *Giving out a phone number is a huge mistake.* Even as a police officer, I would be extremely cautious about giving out my home number to someone I met on the Internet. And since women are more often accosted than men, the idea that my wife might give out her phone number would be even more troubling. If you decide to let your child talk on the phone to someone he met on-line, I would have the child ask for the person's phone number and then call the person from your house, using caller ID blocking. Just to be safe.

The third rule: *If you receive e-mail from a stranger, especially anything X-rated, tell an adult immediately.* The source should be reported to the on-line service and the police at once. Actually, anything a child perceives as odd or over the top should be shared with a parent or teacher right away.

In addition, you should tell your child to trust his instincts. If someone he doesn't know starts asking him a lot of questions, it should set off an alarm. What is it with this person? If someone in real life did that, it would be suspect. The same goes for people on-line. *Anyone pressing a child for information about himself is trouble.*

Numerous news stories about pedophiles connecting with children on-line have created a climate of concern, if not hysteria, among parents about the Internet. Hysteria is not warranted. There are wonderful supports for families in cyberspace itself. Check out the Internet safety links for children, especially **Web Wise Kids** (http://www.web-wisekids.org), which was started by Tracey O'Connell-Jay, whose fourteen-year-old sister disappeared for four months because of an Internet-related connection. Among many other things, Web Wise Kids has clubhouse rules for Internet safety in contract form, which you can download and actually have your child review and sign. Another excellent organization is **CyberAngels**. An adjunct of the Guardian Angels, CyberAngels performs monitoring and educational activities for children on-line. For teens, there is some terrific straight talk to be found at **Live Chat Cyberstreetsmarts** (http://www.cyberangels.org/needhelp/streetsmarts.html).

In truth, a little caution on the Internet goes a long way. Young children who follow the admonitions I have outlined will never be at risk. Teenagers who don't spend their every waking hour surfing around looking for illicit materials and sex conversations will also be fine. If you make certain your children know your rules and follow them, the Internet will be nothing but a marvel for your family.

FILTERING AND BLOCKING SOFTWARE

On the other hand, accidents happen. Just as you can get lost in the real world, you can get lost in cyberspace and mistakenly enter a pretty dark place. It is almost impossible to protect your child with absolute certainty from *accidentally* roaming into an area containing obscene material, but there are measures you can take that will greatly lessen the chances of that ever happening.

Another Predator: Cults

Pedophiles are not the only recruiters on the Internet. Cult members go where the children go, and now cult recruitment is beginning to take on a life in cyberspace. It is crucial that your children understand that one, the computer is real, the people they talk to are real, and the words they exchange can have consequences, and two, you have the right to monitor their friendships and connections on-line. This is not a privacy issue. Just as you have a stake in knowing your children's friends, you also are entitled to knowing whom the child chats with and where. Recently, the cult connections have bloomed into a real business and the cult recruiters are excellent at what they do. Exercise caution, especially if you feel your child might be somewhat vulnerable to enticement.

Pedophiles are to be found all over the Internet, but they are most likely to connect with a child who is tempted or in error ventures into a sex chat room. Most on-line systems have means for parents to control access to different adult-oriented locations, and you can review this with your on-line service provider before you subscribe. For example, America Online and Prodigy have parental controls that restrict certain areas and categories.

Even more effective are software programs. There are many different programs on the market for limiting access to adult places on the Internet, though each of them has a few holes. These programs can be secured free over the Internet or for under $50 in retail stores. To name a few:

Cyber Patrol (http://www.cyberpatrol.com) has a comprehensive list that blocks over 7,500 Internet sources, as of this writing. It can filter any Internet World Wide Web, ftp, Usenet news, gopher, or Internet relay chat site. You can also block off use during certain hours of the day. This software has just about any feature you might want.

CYBERsitter gives the parents the ability to block their children's access to questionable material on the Internet. In other words, you decide what you want to restrict, rather than having it all worked out for you by the software manufacturer. Parents can not only choose to block but can block and alert, and also opt to be alerted when an attempt is made to access an off-limits area. That's pretty neat. It also can protect certain files and particular programs from being accessed.

Net Nanny (http://www.netnanny.com) is also an excellent choice for parents in that it incorporates all of the basic features used in most of the filtering software but also allows the parent a lot of custom options, like stopping a child from using a credit card or from releasing a home phone number. Net Nanny and another program called **Cyber Snoop** let the parent view all of the restricted lists. For the parent who really wants to get into the decision-making aspects of blocking and filtering, these two programs would be ideal, though time-consuming.

SurfWatch (http://www.surfwatch.com) is one of the original filtering systems and it is good for the parent who justs wants basic turn-it-on, switch-it-off service. It doesn't work with America Online, Prodigy, or the Microsoft Network, however.

Other software programs include **X-Stop** (http://www. xstop.com), **Net Shepherd** (http://www.netshepherd.com), **InterGo** (http://www.intergo.com), and **Bess Net** (http:// bess.net).

Even with these filtering devices, an individual can be ambushed by violence or pornography on the computer. A mother in Houston was roaming the "Beanie Baby" category on the Internet and clicked on "Beanie Babies at great prices." Thank goodness her son, who collects the Beanie Babies and often scans the Internet, was not there. Under "Beanie Babies at great prices" were a host of grotesque pornographic images.

Another option for parents is to have their children use Web-based communities like theglobe.com and Talk City. They have supervised chat rooms. Some more inspired families develop their own custom home page with links to various educational sites that are family approved. If you're like me, that might be beyond your technical abilities, but it is an excellent option.

Finally, as you consider what measures are best for your family, you might consult an organization called **Safe-Surf** (http://www.safesurf.com), which works to keep the Internet safe for children. This organization's agenda is to protect children without censorship. As such, they have developed an Internet rating system in collaboration with parents, publishers, providers, and developers. The rating system addresses sexuality and violence and attempts to rank the degree to which the content is sexual or violent. The higher the number, the more disturbing the site might be.

In addition, SafeSurf marks sites on the Internet deemed suitable for children with the SafeSurf Wave, along with listing top sites that are devoted to educating and entertaining children. Microsoft and Netscape both endorse this group, along with 20,000 Internet sites, according to the organization. You can access the SafeSurf page at http://www. safesurf.com/ssplan.html for more information.

OTHER TEMPTATIONS

Another way children can get in trouble on the Internet is shopping for "free" merchandise. Once a name and address is given out for something "free," your child will be on a zillion mailing lists, mostly for unwanted products. A big hook, I know, is the CD of the Month Clubs, which can become a major nuisance and costly to boot.

Again, I would establish firm rules about giving out names and addresses, even for free merchandise. If your child gets an offer that sounds like a dream come true, it's probably just that: a dream with serious strings—make that ropes—attached. I personally make it a policy not to shop on-line yet, because I am not convinced that the privacy of my name or credit card is assured.

TROUBLE ON-LINE

As with any other matter involving your child, open communication is crucial. Listen to your child. Check in with

PROFILE TIPS

Obviously a child should not include her real name or address or phone number in her profile. But predators are clever and experienced at getting information out of children. Children will often reveal their birthdates in their profile. When a predator sees 10/24, he will use that information to figure out that October 24 is her birthday. After chatting with her on-line for a while, the predator might "guess" she sounds like a Scorpio. That "insight" could break down a barrier, which is precisely what the predator wants to do. Children also should never give out their school names or talk about specific local hangouts.

Screen names should not be suggestive. *Hotchik* is going to invite lots of attention, most of which presumably would be unwanted. Find out what your children are using as screen names. You might be surprised.

her frequently. Always encourage your child to let you know if anything odd or troubling occurs when she is on-line. She must grasp that if she is forthcoming with you, whatever happens, you will not blame her or throw the computer out the window. I know a lot of children who've had serious on-line problems and were too scared to mention their concerns to their parents. When that happens, things can escalate without the benefit of your intervention. A little problem can become a serious situation.

If someone is stalking or harassing your child—which, incidentally, is against the law—it should be reported to local law enforcement agencies. But be prudent. A message that reads "Hey, sexy" shouldn't be reported to the police. If an unwanted correspondent should start to stalk or harass your child, tell her to be cool and not to engage him. Silence is a powerful, clear response. It means you don't want to play.

If you sense that something might be going on from your end—that is, your child might be harassing someone or seeking out illicit materials—trust your instincts. We've all been there. We know what it looks and feels like to be hiding something or doing something wrong. If your child behaves suspiciously when you walk into the room, pay attention. She might abruptly shut the computer down or start maniacally using the mouse. She might seem guarded about the computer, resistant to your questions about it. I would have a heart-to-heart at that point. You don't have to accuse your child of anything at first. Just have a conversation about it and enforce stricter limits—and spend more time monitoring the situation.

Whatever you do, make certain your child understands she can talk honestly with you, without fears of being unreasonably punished. Getting help is always a good first step to solving a problem. It is the mark of a child with street smarts.

Chapter 8

STREET SMARTS
FOR TEENS

Parenting is not for the faint of heart. Just when our children figure out how to cross the street safely, they become, of all things, teenagers. Instead of avoiding danger, teenagers seek it out, chasing down wild parties, drugs, alcohol, stupid car tricks, and sexual escapades. A blessed few resist. Some experiment and emerge unscathed. Others don't make it.

This book is not intended to cover the complexities of adolescence. But I did want to include some insights I have gained on the force working with troubled teenagers every day and raising two fine sons. I don't take much credit for my sons. My wife gets the kudos for that. But I do know that because of my job, our children have been raised in an atmosphere of open and frank conversation, and I think it has worked to their advantage. While our sons were growing up, when they asked how my day went, they never knew what they would get: a kinky rape, a kidnapping, or a drug overdose. I didn't dwell on the gore or vulgarity of it, but I also didn't hide much from them. From the get-go, we were honest about naming body parts, sexuality, drinking, and drugs. I believe that our family's openness, which sometimes shocked other parents, allowed us to demonstrate why we set limits. Our sons always accepted our curfews and restrictions (though sometimes begrudgingly). They understood the world as an unpredictable place. Most important, they learned that *actions have real life—or death—consequences.*

This simple but profound connection is lost on most teenagers unless it has been drilled into their heads from a very young age.

Very few children will face the prospect of an abduction. But virtually all teenagers will be faced with the choice of using drugs such as alcohol, nicotine, marijuana, cocaine, heroin, and other chemical substances. They will be faced with the choice of getting into the car with a drunk or reckless driver. They will be faced with decisions about their own sexuality, and the possibility of pregnancy or sexually transmitted diseases, including AIDS.

Most of the professionals I know who work with teens have no simple answers. What we can do is love our children as best we can from the start. We can keep communication lines open. We can make sure there are adults in our children's lives with whom they can be honest, even as they grow away from us. We can give our children the base of a warm, loving family. But even in the best circumstances, children can make mistakes, get sucked into a bad crowd, fall off an emotional ladder, and end up in trouble. When it comes to adolescents, there are no guarantees and a lot of anxiety-filled late nights for parents.

KEEPING THE LINES OPEN

After being sneered at for the fifth time that day, the idea of communicating with our teenagers is pretty low on the list. Who needs it, anyway?

Actually, your child does.

It takes enormous patience to foster communication with a teenager, especially one who is sullen and rude. But the rewards for the child are well worth it. What it takes on your part is hanging back.

These are a few things to keep in mind:

- Listen, listen, listen.
- Don't nag or pester. Save the heavy talk for important issues. Let the little things go.
- Try to remember what being a teenager feels like. Share their reality—don't judge it.
- Always connect privileges with responsibilities.
- Praise them where appropriate. They might shrug it off, but they hear you. (Same goes for a hug.)
- Make only a few rules, and make those rules unbreakable.
- Don't be defensive.
- Let them know you are there for them no matter what; that they can talk with you about anything without fear of judgment.
- Enjoy your life. A child needs to know how fun and enjoyable it is to be an adult, and that you don't need a cigarette and a drink to relax and have a good time.

REAL LIFE 101

From as early as kindergarten, school programs begin to address various teen-related issues such as sexuality and the use of cigarettes, alcohol, and illegal drugs. I have been an active supporter of Wisconsin's DARE Program, and I believe in its value wholeheartedly. With programs like DARE, children in the fifth and sixth grades acquire a sense of what's to come, including peer pressure and how to deal with it, and the dangers and temptations they will face in drug and alcohol abuse.

But there's a catch. The vast majority of fifth graders will tell you fervently how evil cigarettes are and even cite cancer statistics. They will fuss at parents and relatives who smoke and wrinkle their noses when someone lights up in a restaurant. Twenty-four months later you'll find those same kids puffing on a stolen cigarette in the neighborhood alley.

This doesn't mean that drug and alcohol education doesn't work. It just means that many preteens and teenagers are going to experiment, no matter what we say or do. At the very least, they might sneak a beer or try to smoke a cigarette. But without education, our children won't know what they are getting into. They won't understand the very real possibilities of dependency. (It is ironic that at a point when they are trying to assert their independence, adolescents use the only substances upon which they could become *completely* dependent.) Getting the facts is crucial, especially when it comes to addictions. Teenagers won't see the signs in themselves—addicts never do—but they might see the signs in a best friend. Peer pressure works both ways.

In my experience, it often has been a friend who realized that a teenager was in over his head and needed help. If your child has chosen good friends and they are educated about drugs and alcohol, they may save his life.

DANGEROUS PASTIMES

Teenagers use drugs and alcohol for the same reason adults do. Many begin using it for recreation. Others are trying to get rid of the emotional strain and the competitiveness of their lives. (I think it is reasonable to say that our teenagers today are under far more pressure than we experienced growing up.) A good number of teenagers, especially those who start young, use drugs or alcohol to act cool or rebel.

Consumption also varies. Some teenagers have high self-esteem and succeed in not getting involved at all. Others will experiment with drugs or alcohol a couple of times and then decide it's not for them. A large percentage will use small amounts of these substances every now and then, and ultimately quit, finding other means of coping or relaxing. Then there are the teenagers who will get caught and become addicted. If they live, they will face a life centered on overcoming that addiction. In their own minds, they will be so closely identified with drugs or alcohol that a day won't pass where addiction won't be an issue for them—whether they are still using substances or are able to quit.

The stakes, quite obviously, are high. How do you communicate with a teenager who is predisposed to tune you out? Well, for starters, forget the at-home lecture series.

Your teenager will cut you off before you even begin. (Anyway, you probably can't tell him anything he doesn't already know.) But you should keep conversations about drug and alcohol abuse open and constant. You can use a television program as a leaping-off point, whether it's a movie in which kids use drugs or a documentary on the subject. You can ask him what he knows about drugs (he will be much happier to lecture you than to be lectured). You want to keep the facts about addiction in front of your child's face.

The problem is that this brand of information will go only so far in convincing a teenager that drugs and alcohol are not in his best interest. For teenagers, "life is a gas" and "it won't happen to me." Mature individuals know differently, but it is almost impossible to convey that reality to a teenager hellbent on drug or alcohol abuse.

But you can get a teenager's attention. These facts are *not* lost on them:

- Using drugs and alcohol could get him arrested.
- Getting arrested could cost him fines or time in jail or a serious blight on his record.
- He could get very sick, make poor judgments that lead to injury, or die.

Your child needs to know what your policy is on these facts, especially your position on legal matters. Will you bail your child out? Will you pay his fine? Will you go to court and try to have an infraction wiped off his record so he will not lose his chance of getting into a good college? *You have to decide.* My wife and I had a simple policy: You reap what you sow. Our boys knew that if they messed up, they were on their own, whether I was a police officer or not. They had to handle what happened, but we were there to support them.

Another important action a parent can take is to pay attention. In my line of work, I am always looking for clues and signs and contradictions. You don't have to become a detective, but you do need to be observant and willing to act on what you see. Watch your child. Listen to him. If you think your child is in over his head, you will see some of the following signs:

- a change in schoolwork—grades dropping, missing school, cutting classes
- a new group of friends who might be older or from another school
- unusual behavior: more irritable or depressed or combative
- confused or restless, won't look you in the eye
- a need to "be alone" most of the time; lots of time spent in his room away from the family
- getting in trouble at school or in the community
- a new look: different clothing or music tastes
- physical signs: glassy or red eyes, weight loss or gain, fatigue

These are just a few of the flags that might indicate your child is involved with illegal substances. Don't ignore or explain away these symptoms. If it's just part of being a teenager, you'll find that out. If your child has a problem, you may be able to help him turn it around.

If I saw these signs in my child, I would contact a drug and alcohol counselor at once and get professional help. Getting in a knock-down-drag-out fight with your teenager won't solve his problem. Chances are ninety-nine out of a hundred that if you confront your child, he will deny it. You and your child are going to need lots of guidance. In your community, there are many social service agencies and support services you can turn to for help. *This is one operation you shouldn't attempt on your own.*

Also, I would take a look at myself. If you have an alcohol or chemical substance problem, you are a factor in your child's use. You are not totally responsible, but you are part of the equation. Please get help.

TEEN SEXUALITY

All teenagers, even the "good" ones, are far more sexually active and at a far younger age than most of their parents were. The consequences can be unwanted pregnancies, emotional illness, sexually transmitted disease. Every day I come across young teens in trouble. Many were sexually abused as children, and now they act out. I see the extreme cases: promiscuous thirteen-year-old girls with older men, and young boys selling themselves for a five-dollar bill.

As with drugs and alcohol, sexual education is part and parcel of most public school curriculums. Your school will no doubt cover the biology of it all, along with some discussion of abstinence or contraception or both, and of sexually transmitted diseases, including HIV. All of this is very personal and will vary from family to family according to your moral and religious views, but whatever your position, please be open and available to your child on this subject. Among "good" families, I know young women—high school juniors—who take the date rape drug for "fun" at parties. I know sweet, middle-class girls who don't have many friends who get lured into friendships with groups of boys, ending up the victim of a gang rape. I know boys—the jocks, the "good guys"—who have performed sexual "research" on girls and posted ratings of the girls' sexual prowess, leaving the girls humilated and emotionally damaged.

It is very difficult for me to overstate the degree to which teenagers are sexually active and the variety of practices and abuses that have resulted from all of this.

Where does street smarts come in?

Again, the first and most important thing you can do is to get real. Be aware. Find out what is really happening in your community. Talk to your pediatrician. Talk to your local birth control agency. Speak to parents of older children. Find out what is happening at your child's middle and high school.

Then you must decide how to approach your child's sexuality. Again, this is an extremely personal issue. I can do no more than emphasize that you need to think about your child's sexuality well before you even dream it might become an issue. You need to decide how you will counsel your child with respect to birth control and/or abstinence.

And yes, you need to communicate with your child and be there for him or her every step of the way.

THE AWFUL TRUTH ABOUT TEENAGE DRIVERS

The number-one killer of teenagers is car accidents. We read about them in the news every day. You may even know a family that has lost a teenager to a tragic accident. As many years as I have been in the force, I still blanch when I hear over the police radio that a teen has been killed on the highway. Another grim fact: One out of five car deaths occur when a teenager is driving, though teenagers represent only 5 percent of the driving population.

NO QUESTIONS ASKED

Your child is going to face a lot of tricky situations before he becomes an adult. If he is at a party that is getting dangerously out of hand, he should know he can call you for a pickup, no questions asked. If he is drunk and can't drive, he should be able to call for help and get it without a lecture on the ride home. (Hold off. You'll obviously want to chat, but wait until he's sobered up.) I would strongly recommend instituting the "no questions asked" policy for every potentially dangerous situation, so that no matter what, your child can turn to you in an emergency without fear of reprisal.

Road smarts are a function of experience. Teenagers don't have experience. Many of them also lack common sense. You have to decide what your family policy is going to be about allowing your child to drive and allowing him to ride with others.

Some families, for example, require their children to wait until they have a driver's license before allowing them to ride with another teen driver (on the theory that they could take over the wheel if the driver was impaired in some manner). Other families have their teens wait until six months after their friend has obtained a license to ride with that friend, believing that six months of driving will give the friend some semblance of experience.

Whatever you do, don't just sit back and wish for the best. To that end:

- Start your teen driving as soon as possible. Practice around the neighborhood or in parking lots or on empty country roads.
- Limit the first months of your teen's driving to the daytime. Also, do not let her on the highways in her first months of driving.
- Don't start off letting your child drive around with a full load of passengers. Passengers can easily distract new drivers. For the first months, she should be limited to a small number—or no—passengers. Also, thinking ahead, figure out what kind of weather you will allow her to drive in. Storms can be extremely dangerous.
- Determine what you will require for her to have the

privilege of her driver's license: She must wear a seat belt, drive sober, stay free of speeding or traffic violations. Decide how long her driving privileges will be suspended if she fails to honor your safe-driving rules.
- Coach her on what to do if she gets in an accident.
- Teach her how to change a flat tire.

WALKING THE WALK

By the time he is a teenager, the street-smart child is also wise; he retains an instinct for self-preservation and draws strength from a sense of his own innate dignity. Guiding teenagers while letting them grow is the greatest challenge for parents.

When your child was young, you could get away with a lot of imperfections and even hypocrisy. That no longer is the case. "Do as I say, not as I do" isn't going to cut it with the defiant teenager. This goes for the obvious—safe driving, smoking, drinking, using illegal drugs—and the not so obvious: the father who stays late at the office and doesn't call in, the mother who buckles to social peer pressures. It's unfair, perhaps, but who ever promised fair?

If you don't buckle your seat belt, you can bet your child won't buckle hers. If you drink every day, nobody's going to listen to you pontificate about alcohol. If you smoke cigarettes, the chances of your child smoking just doubled. If you smoke marijuana . . . well, you're probably not reading this book, so never mind.

If you want your child to be assertive in negative peer

pressure situations, don't act like a doormat when a bossy relative tries to take advantage of your goodwill or when the volunteer chair calls you for the four hundredth time to run the school carnival. Say no, rather than complain about how you get stuck with it every year. If an aggressive salesperson starts pressuring you to buy something, and you don't want it, decline. Let your child hear you say no firmly and politely.

Finally, radiate your own uniqueness with confidence. Teenagers want to be respected as individuals by their peers, but they don't want to be too different. If there is negative peer pressure, this can be a terrible trap even for the adolescent who wants to do the right thing. If your family is locked into conformist behavior, dress, and activities, you may be perpetuating the subconscious fears your child has of being different. Show your child that being different won't subject him to ridicule. Try, in your own life, to think outside the box a little bit. Pursue an interest that is uniquely your own; plan a trip to an exotic place so your child can see that there's a world outside of his zip code.

Last and not least, treat your teenager with respect. That's probably the most powerful thing you can do as a parent and as a human being.

Chapter 9

STREET SMARTS Q & A

I spend a lot of time with parents, and over the years I have found their concerns to be remarkably consistent. That being the case, I am including in this book some of the questions I am most frequently asked when I give a talk about street smarts. Use this chapter to test and refresh yourself and your child on the mechanics of safety. Some of this information I have covered in previous chapters of the book. But remember, with street smarts, a single lecture or talk with your child will never be as effective as ongoing discussions. Your goal is to train your child with repetition and intelligent reminders. Don't nag and don't do all of the talking. And sometimes, as obvious as it sounds, why not listen?

Rather than lecture, be creative. Play the "what if" game or have your child "teach" a younger sibling how to cross the street. If a tragedy is reported in the newspaper, discuss it with your child along with what choices a child could have made to avert the situation. Even teenagers (perhaps, *especially* teenagers) should be briefed and subject to "reviews," particularly if they are experiencing a first trip or unsupervised outing that could put them at risk.

One family I know created a little "safety club" for their eight-year-old son. After school on Thursdays, about ten of his buddies came over for a snack and a safety talk. The mother enlisted guest speakers—a fireman and a police officer—and she had them do drills and role playing, everything from answering the door to putting a bandage on. The boys went on a bicycle hike, to practice on-the-street safety. They went to a mall and talked about what to do if they got lost or separated. The children met for ten weeks and loved it. In the end they had a "drill" and showed their parents all that they had learned. The moms and dads learned more in that single presentation than they had known about safety all of their parenting lives.

There are many creative ways to approach teaching street smarts. The key is: Just do it, and do it often. Here are some basics every parent and child should know.

How do I teach my child to cross a street safely?

"Look both ways" still applies. Look left, right, and then left again. Alert your child to the fact that even if the light at a crosswalk says "walk," drivers who are not paying attention might round a corner and invade the walking path. *Street-smart children never make assumptions, no matter what a sign or light says.* Point out painted crosswalks on streets with the same warning. Just because the light says "walk" or there is a crosswalk there, doesn't mean drivers are aware of it. The pedestrian has to be aware at all times and proceed based on his own assessment of the situation.

What are some ways to prepare my child for walking to school?

When walking alone, a street-smart child looks around and stays aware of what is happening. He walks confidently in the middle of the sidewalk and avoids shortcuts, especially rarely traveled alleys and vacant lots.

If the child has a routine for walking home from school, he should know safe houses along the way—whether it is the public library or a neighbor. Walk the route *with him* several times and quiz him on safe places. Point out hidden driveways where cars might emerge out of nowhere.

If a stranger is approaching him face-to-face, the child should stay a safe distance—at least three feet—from that person when he passes him on the sidewalk. If he feels he is being followed, he should run to a safe house.

It is always better for a child to walk with a friend—the more buddies, the safer he will be—no matter where he is going.

I worry about my three-year-old. She wanders off in a split second. Should I just avoid public places with her?

I get variations on this question all of the time. Sometimes the "escape artist" is a toddler. Other times it is a retarded child who wants to explore. Another problem that comes up—especially when I am talking with mothers—is not so much the wandering child but the lackadaisical husband who isn't tuned in to the fine art of paying attention. Many moms are afraid to let their husbands take a child to the park or a fast-food place, and in some cases, I don't blame them.

The last thing I want to do is get in between a husband and wife on the subject of child-rearing, but I will say that men as a rule are not as *naturally* tuned in to the task of watching small children. I wince when I see men in malls "leading" their small children, who invariably get distracted and "fall out of line." Small children need to be watched. Retarded children with a predisposition to get distracted or run away need to be watched like a hawk. I would not avoid public places—all of these children need to learn how to function in them—but I would make sure they have the best supervision possible, even if that means tagging along with a husband who is more casual about the process.

All children, as soon as they are able, need to know their names and addresses, phone numbers, and parents' names, and how to use a pay telephone. They need to know to call 911 in an emergency. They need to know to go to a person in uniform or a person wearing a store apron or name tag if they are lost. They should never wander around looking for you, or leave the mall, go to the parking lot to your car, or hide if afraid. When you are going to a public place, identify a meeting area in case children get separated from the group—whether you are in a familiar shopping center or grocery store or in a museum you've never been to.

As a parent, I would also accompany my child on field trips from school whenever possible, and make sure that the teacher has instructed the children about all of the above.

It always surprises me that elementary and middle schools do not prepare children for field trips with basic safety strategies.

What are the pros and cons of a family code word?

The family code word is an agreed-upon word (pet name, sports team name, whatever) that children are to use as a password if an adult wants to take them somewhere. If little Susie is not expecting Mrs. Jones to pick her up after school, and Mrs. Jones insists that Susie's mom asked her to, Susie asks for the code word. If Mrs. Jones can produce it, Susie theoretically knows it is safe to proceed with the woman.

I recommend the family code word because I have seen it work effectively in dozens of cases, saving children from heading off with an adult who is up to no good. Here's why it is good: For one thing, it makes children think before they act and realize that there are some people in their lives who can be trusted (those who know the code) and some who *cannot*. If a child knows to go only with those who know the family code word, you have for the most part eliminated strangers from taking your child. The problem is that in an emergency, children panic, forget to use the code word, or might blurt it out upon request (a tactic used by some adults who "test" the child to avoid being tested *by* the child). The other problem is that children sometimes forget the code word, especially if the family changes it frequently. (Once Mrs. Jones in the previous example knows Susie's code word, Susie's family might think they should change it for security reasons. You thus might be changing it constantly, which seems unnecessary to me.)

The family code word will work if you stress that it should be kept secret and also review the use of the word on a repeat basis. Telling the child the family code word once and never bringing it up again is completely ineffective.

How old should my child be before I let him walk alone to school or go to the mall with friends and unaccompanied by an adult?

If all children were the same, I could answer this question so easily. But there is no easy way to answer this question.

You need to assess your child's ability to respond on his own to a variety of situations before making a decision as to whether he is able to navigate his way to school or through a mall or other public place. Again, playing the "what if" game is a perfect way to measure your child's common sense. Remember, what he knows he will have learned primarily from you. Your ability to train the child and his ability to absorb the training is the most important aspect of letting your child go off on his own.

For instance, a child is who learning to walk to school should be able to absorb all of the basics presented in this book (see pages 31-33 for details). But you might also go one step further and test him. One mother I know "set up" her child on his first trial run and had someone approach her child in a car to ask for directions, just to test his response. (He fled the driver, which gave the mother enormous peace of mind.)

As far as going to a shopping mall or arcade or other public place without an adult, I see children of all ages permitted this freedom. If a parent has prepared her child properly, if the child knows what to do if lost or separated from friends and the kinds of lures from strangers to avoid, she might be ready to go with friends. I would be far more comfortable the first dozen or so times being present on the premises (movie theater, mall, and so forth) and arranging for meeting times. Abductors mill around where children hang out. Age is no protection.

What should a child do if he is being mugged?

This is a problem, especially for children in urban areas. I know that in New York City, many of the private school kids take off their uniforms and put on casual clothes before going home, so as not to attract attention from gangs. Your child should always know to hand over whatever a mugger demands. The only time he should resist is if an abduction is also attempted. He should never get into a car with a mugger and should run and scream as loud as he can. (Remember to tell your child to yell in a deep voice, for as long as he can hold it.) If a mugging has taken place, he should report it to a trusted adult or the police as soon as possible.

What are the main elements of bicycle safety?

About 90 percent of the head injuries that occur could have been prevented if the child had been wearing a helmet. So the first thing I would offer is that the helmet is not negotiable. If your child wants to ride his bicycle, he wears the helmet, whether it is cool or not.

A street-smart parent will hold a child back from riding

her bike alone until the child shows that she knows the law. She should learn the following:

- Use proper hand signals when making turns. (If you are turning right, the arm is raised in a Native American "how" position. If you are turning left, the arm is extended straight out.)
- Look left, then right, then left again when riding into traffic from a sidewalk, driveway, or parking lot.
- Come to a complete stop at stop signs.
- On the street, ride single file. Most cities have laws on how far you can ride from the curb (generally, three feet).
- Avoid riding your bike at dusk when visibility is low.
- Again, always wear a bike helmet.

People often want to know how old a child should be before you can allow him to ride his bicycle alone. This is a developmental rather than chronological issue. Most elementary schools require a child to be in third or fourth grade before riding her bike to school.

What about car safety?

Obviously, all people need to wear a seat belt. When putting on a seat belt, pull it tight, and if the shoulder strap comes across your neck or face, tuck it behind your back.

- Never throw anything in a car. You may hit the driver and cause an accident.

- Do not yell in a car. It might scare the driver.
- Don't ride in the front passenger seat unless you are twelve years of age due to the presence of the air bag, which if deployed could cause harm.
- Parents should use child locks until children are responsible enough not to fiddle with car doors.

We just bought a house that has a pool. We have three little children, and now I am a nervous wreck about the possibility of drowning.

Swimming pools can be danger zones for children—there's no doubt about it. Every year more than 350 children under the age of five drown in residential swimming pools. Two thousand more are treated for injuries sustained in backyard pools. Since 1980, more than 200 children under five have drowned in hot tubs. The tragic part is that in the vast majority of cases when these accidents occurred, the child was being supervised by at least one adult—but the child wasn't supposed to be in or near the pool. If you have a pool, you have a huge responsibility to protect not only your own children but also their friends and even the neighbor's child who might wander into your yard.

Most cities require fencing around pools to protect children. The fences help, but children often learn how to open gates before their parents are aware that they have the dexterity to do so. If you have a gate that is supposed to close on its own, make certain it is hinged so that it closes securely. Self-locking and self-closing gates are a must. If I still had small children, even if they knew how to swim, I would have the gate locked at all times. No exceptions.

Obviously, the quicker you can get your children swimming, the more peace of mind you will have, and children can learn how to "save themselves"—that is, find their way to the edge of the pool—at a fairly young age. Also, be practical. If you are outside with the children, take the phone with you or decide you will just let the answering machine take calls. Children drown in minutes.

It goes without saying, but I'll say it: Never allow a child to swim alone.

If a child is drowning, especially in a river or lake, don't jump in at once. If possible, offer a long pole to her or throw a life preserver. If no implement is available you obviously need to go in after her, but exercise caution. I've seen numerous cases of multiple drownings whereby the rescuer lost her life in the process of trying to save someone. I also stress the importance for adults in charge to know CPR. This means parents, caregivers, or anyone who is going to be responsible for your children.

How do you know if a coach or camp counselor is safe? How do you check them out?

First, let me underline the importance of checking out anyone who is going to be working with your child. References are key. If it is a coach, ask for the names of team parents with whom he or she has previously worked. For camp counselors, find out how long they have been at the camp, whom they have worked with before, and whether they have hopscotched from camp to camp, especially from state to state. (Child molesters, especially those with convictions, often change states to avoid being identified.) When you interview parents, ask open-ended questions; don't prompt them. Linger on the phone. Allow for some silences, which people will sometimes out of nervousness fill in and reveal an important fact.

Second, make sure your child is sensitive to behavior that might be out of line. Your child should know it is his right and obligation to report anything strange or discomforting about this person.

What is the most important thing I can teach my child to prevent her from ever being abducted?

For me, the most important habit a child can get into is to always ask a parent for permission to go anywhere. Children are impetuous. They disappear. They run off to the rest room or down an aisle in a store to view some toys or over to a neighbor's without thinking to tell anyone. It is in these moments that most children are alone and unsupervised and vulnerable to abductors. Even your teenagers should know not to go anywhere without telling you. If you begin the habit at an early age, you safeguard your child immeasurably.

Also, a child should know not to judge by appearances. Strangers most often don't look like the stereotype of a molester or abductor. They often are well dressed and friendly. *This doesn't mean they are safe.* A child also should never accept a stranger's request for help.

How can I talk to my three-year-old about sexual abuse?

You can start by teaching your child his or her body parts, using the correct anatomical names, from the very beginning. You can also teach your child to let you know anytime he feels uncomfortable with an adult or another child—so that he knows he can advocate for himself. Build his self-esteem so that he knows he is a dignified human being who under no circumstances should be violated or compromised in any way.

The most crucial part of teaching children about sexual abuse is not so much sex education per se—though children should be knowledgeable about their own sexuality—but the ability of your child to communicate with you. Your child needs to understand that you are there for him in many ways. If a child knows he is loved unconditionally, he will share his feelings and report anything that might be amiss without feeling too embarrassed or ashamed. Children must be taught never to keep secrets from their parents.

Many parents clam up when they need to address sexual topics with their children—when a straightforward, matter-of-fact approach is actually easy to execute, *especially* if you begin talking with your children about it at a young age.

LAST WORD

As parents, we are always treading that fine line between concern for the safety of our children and flat-out paranoia. Given that I spend all day with victims, I should fall into the latter category. Sometimes, after a particularly grueling day, I find it hard to remember that most people are decent, good, law-abiding citizens. And that, in fact, is the truth. Most people *are* decent. Crimes against children are executed by the terrible few, and many of these crimes can be stopped or prevented. In most cases, children are victims because someone looked the other way or failed to heed a warning.

"Street smarts" isn't just a catchy phrase. It's the wisdom common to all ages, because, unfortunately, as many advances as we have made, human nature hasn't changed since the beginning of time. But in law enforcement, we are learning more about the way things work, the way criminals operate, the way accidents happen, and the means to make the world a much safer place. I'm optimistic, and you should be too.

Keep safe, and say hello to the family for me.

To send questions or safety tips to Detective Ric Bentz, write care of The Kenosha Police Department, 1000 55th Street, Kenosha, WI 53140.

FOR MORE
INFORMATION

In the course of doing research for this book, I read a lot
and referred to other books on the subject. These included:
*Safe and Sound: Protecting Your Child in an Unpredictable
World* by Vanessa L. Ochs (Penguin, 1995); *Child Lures:
What Every Parent and Child Should Know About Preventing
Sexual Abuse and Abduction* by Kenneth Wooden (Summit
Publishing Group, 1995); *Raising Safe Kids in an Unsafe
World: 30 Simple Ways to Prevent Your Child from Being Lost,
Abducted, or Abused* by Jan Wagner and Seth Goldstein
(Avon Books, 1996).

Below is a list of books you might use directly with your
child. I suggest you peruse these books at the library or
bookstore before reading them to or with your child. In
some cases, the material is sensitive and you may find the
approach unsuitable. The only books I would strongly suggest parents avoid are those that encourage parents to develop "escape" plans or martial art self-defense skills for
abduction situations. When you emphasize escape training for children—such as how to get out of a locked car

trunk—you arouse unnecessary fear. Escape techniques also require numerous weeks of training and constant review. I believe the emphasis should rest on avoiding danger in the first place. The smartest kids can sense danger and avoid it. In addition, I personally believe that only the very rare child could be trained to overcome an adult in a physical contest. A child should not engage a predator in combat, but flee.

Here are some reading possibilities for your child: *Be Aware of Danger* by Bill Gutman (Twenty-First Century Books, 1996), age 9–12; *It's My Body* by Lory Freeman and Carol Deach (Parenting Press, 1983); *My Body Is Private* by Linda Walvoord Girard and Rodney Pate (Albert Whitman & Co., 1987), ages 4–8; *The Safe Zone: A Kid's Guide to Personal Safety* by Donna Chaiet et al. (William Morrow, 1998), ages 9–12; *Your Body Belongs to You* by Cornelia Spelman and Teri Weidner (Albert Whitman & Co., 1997).

I included numerous sources for help in protecting children from the various ills of the Internet. The Internet, nonetheless, is a fabulous source of safety information. Any search engine can turn up tens of thousands of files on child safety.

In addition, there are agencies you might like to contact for further information on this subject. Here are a few for your files:

American Academy of Pediatrics
141 Northwest Point Boulevard
P.O. Box 927
Elk Grove Village, IL 60009
847-228-5005
800-433-9016

American Red Cross National Headquarters
17th and D Streets N.W.
Washington, DC 20006

Child Quest International
1625 The Alameda
Suite 400
San Jose, CA 95126
408-287-HOPE
800-248-8020 (call for sightings)

Council on Family Health
225 Park Avenue South, Suite 1700
New York, NY 10003
212-598-3617

Food and Drug Administration
5600 Fishers Lane
Room 16-85
Rockville, MD 20857
301-443-3170

Juvenile Products Manufacturers Association
236 Route 38 West, Suite 100
Moorestown, NJ 08057
609-231-8500

National Center for Missing and Exploited Children
2101 Wilson Boulevard
Suite 550
Arlington, VA 22201
703-235-3900
800-THE-LOST (call for sightings)

National Child Pornography Tip Line
800-843-5678

National Fire Protection Association
Batterymarch Park
Quincy, MA 02269-9101
617-770-3000
617-328-9290

National Safe Kids Campaign
111 Michigan Avenue, N.W.
Washington, DC 20010
202-884-4993

National Safety Council
1121 Spring Lake Drive
Itasca, IL 60143
Central region 800-621-7619
Northeastern region 800-432-5251
Southeastern region 800-441-5103
Western region 800-848-5588

The Polly Klaas Foundation
P.O. Box 800
Petaluma, CA 94953
800-587-HELP

United States Consumer Product Safety Commission
4330 East West Highway
Bethesda, MD 20814
301-504-0550
800-638-CPSC

INDEX

ABOUT THE AUTHORS

Detective RIC BENTZ has been a member of the Kenosha Police Department since 1977. He is currently the coordinator of the Sensitive Crimes Unit, specializing in the prevention of missing and exploited children. He lives in Wisconsin with his wife and two sons.

CHRISTINE ALLISON is the author of nonfiction books, including parenting titles. She is a regular contributor to *Reader's Digest*. She lives in Texas with her husband and four daughters.

LOOK FOR THESE *NEW YORK TIMES* BESTSELLERS:

REVIVING OPHELIA
Saving the Selves of Adolescent Girls
by Mary Pipher, Ph.D.

"An important book . . .
Pipher shines high-beam headlights
on the world of teenage girls."
—*Los Angeles Time*s

****

RAISING CAIN
Protecting the Emotional Life of Boys
by Dan Kindlon, Ph.D., and Michael Thompson, Ph.D.

"*Raising Cain* gives a long-needed insight into that myste-
rious, magical land, the psyches of boys. Every parent,
teacher—or anyone who wants boys to flourish—should
read this book."
—DANIEL GOLEMAN
Author of *Emotional Intelligence*

Available in bookstores everywhere.
Published by Ballantine Books
The Ballantine Publishing Group
www.randomhouse.com/BB/

And don't miss this essential resource for
raising your kids:

PARENTING YOUR TEENAGER
by David Elkind, Ph.D.

AIDS. Violence. Drinking. Drugs.
If you think your teenager is sophisticated
about these issues,
think again. . . .

Dr. David Elkind, child psychologist and author of the
renowned child development classic *The Hurried Child*,
understands today's teenagers. He knows that teenagers are
not the cool know-it-alls the media makes them out to be,
but sensitive, anxious, often troubled youngsters who still
rely on their parents for moral guidance, emotional support,
and sound rules and values. In *Parenting Your Teenager*, Dr.
Elkind draws on his extensive knowledge of adolescent development to provide practical advice on all the tough challenges and choices that teenagers and their parents face.
Compassionate, informative, and engagingly written, this
wonderful book helps all parents rise to the special challenges of guiding their adolescent children into maturity.